HOW TO FLY A
BATTLE OF BRITAIN
FIGHTER

SPITFIRE MESSERSCHMITT HURRICANE

HOW TO FLY A
BATTLE OF BRITAIN
FIGHTER

SPITFIRE MESSERSCHMITT HURRICANE

Ed. Campbell McCutcheon

Spitfire (5 March 1936). The Messerschmitt was designed by two men, Willy Messerschmitt himself and Robert Lusser, an engineer who had worked for Heinkel and Klemm before joining the Bavarian aircraft factory that produced the Messerschmitt fighter.

The Spitfire's designer was R. J. Mitchell, who would die sixteen months after the first flights were made by K5054, the prototype aircraft. Mitchell had designed the Schneider Trophy entrants for Supermarine as well as flying boats and seaplanes such as the Walrus and Stranraer. In all, some twenty-four designs can be attributed to Mitchell, who died, aged 42, of cancer. Development work took place on the Spitfire which pushed its life over fourteen years at a time when jets were beginning to enter service in huge numbers.

Hawker's chief designer was Sydney Camm, and he was responsible for many designs from the 1920s right into the jet age. Camm was responsible for many of the aircraft used by the RAF through the 1930s, including the previous generation of fighter, the Hawker Hart. He had a hand in some fifty-six different aircraft designs, of which over 26,000 different models flew. His Typhoon and Tempest designs were also outstanding.

Messerschmitt Bf 109

The first of the three to fly, the Messerschmitt Bf 109 was an all-metal monocoque, powered by a V12 aero engine. It had originally been conceived as an interceptor but developments in the design and the needs of the Luftwaffe saw it used as a fighter bomber, bomber escort, ground-attack and a reconnaissance aircraft. Messerschmitt themselves built 33,984 109s, and 239 HA-1112 and 603 Avia S-199s were built under licence too.

Germany's top scoring aces all flew 109s for most, if not all, of their flying careers on the Eastern Front, with some 928 victories between them. The Messerschmitt was also used by the Finnish, Italian, Romanian, Croatian, Bulgarian and Hungarian air forces.

First conceived in 1933 as a proposal to replace the Heinkel and Arado biplanes then in service, the brief was for a fighter that could fly at 400 km/h at 6,000 metres, with a ninety-minute endurance. Arado, Heinkel and Bayerische Flugzeugwerke all proposed designs for the Luftwaffe. Development work began in March 1934 and a mock-up was ready by January 1935. By May 1935, the prototype was ready but the engines were not. The Germans did a deal with Rolls-Royce to supply four engines in exchange for a Heinkel He 70 that could be used as an engine test bed and the Messerschmitt first flew with a Rolls-Royce Kestrel engine at the end of May 1935. By October, another Messerschmitt Bf 109 was flying with a Junkers Jumo engine. In February 1936, the Arado Ar 80, Focke-Wulf Fw 159, Heinkel He 112 and Bf 109 were flying against each other. The Messerschmitt was simply a better aircraft than the Arado and Focke-Wulf entries and they were soon discounted. The Messerschmitt was 20 mph faster than the Heinkel, was superior in its handling and was soon chosen over the Heinkel as the aircraft of choice for the Luftwaffe. During the Berlin Olympics in the summer of 1936, the Messerschmitt made its first public appearance. By this time, the Spitfire had already been accepted by the RAF.

The Messerschmitt was designed cleverly so that its wings did not contain the undercarriage. This meant they needed less loading, could be made lighter and the aircraft could be kept on its undercarriage even with the wings removed. This did lead to a narrow track, which caused some issues with stability when landing, taxiing and taking off, but the ease of repair and maintenance outweighed these problems.

In the original Messerschmitt design, the weapons were located on the fuselage, with two machine guns firing through the propeller, and it was designed to have a cannon firing through the propeller boss too. With the news that the Spitfire would have eight wing-mounted guns, the Messerschmitt was redesigned to take one gun on each wing, which could be either a 20 mm cannon or a 7.62 mm machine gun. By the 109F variant, the wing guns were mounted on pods under each wing.

On 11 November 1937, a Bf 109 with a racing engine flew at a speed of 379.38 mph, breaking the speed record for piston-engined landplanes. For the first time, Germany had a world-beating aircraft. Until the advent of the Focke-Wulf Fw 190, the Messerschmitt 109 was the only single-engined fighter used by the Luftwaffe. Fully a third of all Messerschmitts built were Bf 109Gs but the ones used in the Battle of Britain were the 109E and the 109F. During the war, some 30,573 Messerschmitt 109s were built of all variants, and after the war 865 109Gs were built in Czechoslovakia as the Avia S-99 and S-199, with production stopping in 1948. The Spanish air force used many German aircraft, built in Spain under licence, and the last Messerschmitt 109 was built in 1958.

Used in the Spanish Civil War, the Messerschmitt first saw combat there, and was actively used in all of the German campaigns during the war, from Poland to North Africa. The 109 can claim more kills than any other aircraft of the war, and probably in the lifetime of aerial warfare too. 105 pilots were credited with over 100 kills each, thirteen of those with over 200 and two with more than 300. In the Battle of Britain, the Messerschmitt saw much active service and was a match for the Spitfire and Hurricane.

Supermarine Spitfire

With its first flight on 5 March 1936, the Supermarine Spitfire was designed by R. J. Mitchell, using his experience of the air-speed record breaking Schneider Trophy racers of the late 1920s and early 1930s. The strong airframe could cope with a variety of Rolls-Royce engines from the 1,030 hp Merlin to the 2,340 hp Griffon, giving the Spitfire a long and useful career, and making it the only British fighter aircraft to be built before, during and after the war and in a range of variants from fighters to reconnaissance variants, with a Seafire version that could fly from aircraft carriers too.

The Spitfire was a direct result of Air Ministry Specification F7/30 of 1931, which ultimately saw the biplane Gloster Gladiator accepted into service in the mid-1930s. By 1935, a new specification, F10/35, was created, and designed around Mitchell's Type 300 aircraft. The Air Ministry funded the construction of a prototype and on 5 March 1936 it made its first flight from Eastleigh, the closest airfield to Supermarine's Woolston factory. With an eight-minute initial flight, the test pilot, Captain Joseph Summers, simply said 'Don't touch anything' upon landing the superb new fighter. By mid-May 1936, the Spitfire's speed was nudging 350 mph and the aircraft was handed over to the RAF for evaluation. Within a fortnight, orders for 310 Spitfires were given to Supermarine. By the end of June, at Hendon, the Spitfire made its public appearance. Supermarine's Woolston factory could not cope with the construction of the aircraft and the first RAF production models did not reach service until May 1938, but orders for another 200 had already been made in March, as a result of the deteriorating political situation in Europe. The situation in Europe had been foreseen and the Air Ministry had planned a series of factories throughout the country that could build both fighters and bombers. These 'shadow' factories were built by Austin, including one at Castle Bromwich, in the West Midlands, where the majority of Spitfires would ultimately be produced. By June 1940, production at Castle Bromwich was beginning and the factory would ultimately build over 10,000 Spitfires.

On 23 August 1940, bombs dropped on Woolston and Itchen in an effort to halt Spitfire production in Southampton. Dispersal of production tools had already taken place and despite both factories being wrecked in September 1940, Spitfire construction continued.

The design of the Spitfire gave it a distinctive silhouette and the elliptical wings its most distinctive feature. With four machine guns in each wing, the Spitfire was also well-armed, although a shortage of Browning machine guns saw four fitted per aircraft initially until production of these weapons began to flow. During the Battle of Britain, the Spitfire became an icon for Britain's stand against Nazi Germany, with Lord Beaverbrook organizing Spitfire Funds to pay for Spitfires. Despite being outnumbered by the Hurricane, the Spitfire was the 'sexier' aircraft and its higher performance and lower casualty rate saw it become an iconic aircraft. Its constant development and continued production saw it used in high speed tests, with one variant reaching Mach 0.92 in high speed dive tests, the fastest speed accurately recorded in a piston-engined aircraft. The highest a Spitfire reached was over 50,000 feet in 1952.

Spitfires were produced in twenty-four marks, including carrier-borne versions and high-speed photo-reconnaissance versions. Used post-war in the Malayan Emergency, the last operation flight of a Spitfire was in 1954, from RAF Seletar. Spitfires were still in service in Syria in 1953.

Hawker Hurricane

The plane that saved Britain during the 1940 Battle of Britain, and which accounted for over 60 per cent of British victories in the Battle, was the Hurricane. Overshadowed by the more famous Messerschmitt and Spitfire fighters, it was nonetheless a competent and robust design. Perhaps not as modern as the two monocoques, it was still a revolutionary design, strong and safe, and an excellent gun platform.

Hawker aircraft had provided the mainstay of the RAF's fighter squadrons since the end of the First World War and the Hurricane, like the Spitfire, was developed out of Air Ministry specification F7/30. By January 1935, Hawker had completed a preliminary wooden mock-up of the Hurricane and the first prototype was built and flown by November 1935. In February 1936, the prototype was handed over to the RAF. Its design was still set in the 1920s, with wooden formers and a doped linen skin. By late 1939, all wings were of duralumin construction and metal covered. The aircraft was designed by Sydney Camm with excellent visibility. The fabric design of the fuselage meant that cannon shells could pass through the body without exploding, and the Hurricane was more easily repaired using tools typically found on an airfield. Both Spitfire and Messerschmitt required more complicated jigs to repair damaged bodies. A Hurricane's wings could also be changed in less than three hours, meaning damaged aircraft could be back in action very quickly.

On 12 October 1937, the first production Hurricane flew and in December the first four entered active service. By the outbreak of war, almost 500 Hurricanes were in service with eighteen squadrons. A Hurricane could be constructed more simply in 50 per cent less time than a Spitfire and repaired more easily when damaged. The stable platform and robustness saw it used in many theatres of the war. Hawker themselves constructed nearly 10,000, with Gloster making 2,750 and Austin making another 300. In Canada, another 1,400 Hurricanes were made.

On 21 October 1939, the Hurricane first saw action, when A Flight of 46 Squadron encountered nine Heinkel He 115B floatplanes. Four of the Heinkels were shot down by Hurricanes with another two lost to Spitfires. Four squadrons of Hurricanes saw service in France from September 1939, with two more arriving later in the year. They saw action extensively during the Battle of France in May and June 1940. The battle-hardened Luftwaffe pilots inflicted heavy casualties during the Blitzkrieg but, by the time of the evacuation from Dunkirk, the Hurricane pilots had found their feet and twenty-seven Hurricane pilots became aces during Operation Dynamo.

During the Battle of Britain, Hurricanes accounted for 55 per cent of German losses, with the Spitfires downing 42 per cent. This can be accounted for in the fact that the Hurricanes often targeted the bombers while the Spitfires attacked their fighter escorts, but in a dog fight, the Hurricane could also out turn a Messerschmitt. The construction meant they could survive an attack that a Messerschmitt or Spitfire couldn't but also caused problems with fire, as did the forward-mounted fuel tank, which could burn a pilot if set on fire.

Only one Victoria Cross was awarded to a Battle of Britain pilot, Flt Lt Eric Nicolson, flying a Hurricane with 249 Squadron. After the

Battle of Britain, the Hurricane proved an excellent night fighter and shot down many German bombers during the Blitz that followed. In North Africa and the defence of Malta, the Hurricane saw much service and 2,952 Hurricanes were also sent to Russia. In the Far East, Hurricanes saw service as they did, from 1941, aboard aircraft carriers as the Sea Hurricane. Older Hurricanes were also converted for catapult launching from merchant ships on Russian convoys. Designed for a single flight, these were used to chase away enemy bombers and reconnaissance aircraft during the convoy voyages past the tip of Norway into Murmansk and Archangel.

Numerous other countries flew the Hurricane and it perversely saw action in both Allied and Axis air forces. Air forces which used the Hurricane included Yugoslav, Finnish, Romanian and Polish as well as the Belgian, Canadian, Australian, Greek and Turkish air forces.

Which Was Best?

The arguments over which of these three aircraft was the superior will probably run on and on. Everyone has their favourite, but the numbers speak for themselves during the Battle of Britain. Numerically, the Hurricane shot down more enemy aircraft than either the Messerschmitt or the Spitfire. The publicity surrounding it and the fund-raising drives to pay for Spitfires saw them become more famous, both at the time and to the present day.

The Hurricane was quintessentially British – rugged, dependable, predictable – while the Spitfire was also typically British – distinctive, cleverly designed and beautiful to behold. The Messerschmitt itself was more workmanlike and most definitely Germanic. Within the following pages, the original pilot's notes for the Spitfire and Hurricane are reprinted in their entirety while the original Air Ministry notes on flights based on captured Messerschmitt 109s are also reproduced. Unlike the reams of documentation that would come with a modern jet aircraft, these simple books provide the basics for a budding fighter pilot and contained all one needed to know to be able to fly a Battle of Britain fighter. The true skill came not in the basic flying but the ability to survive against the odds when being shot at. For that we must be thankful that The Few were such fantastic aviators, for without them, the world would have been a much different place. Judge for yourself which was the best.

Photographed from another Bf 109, a Spitfire has
a bogey on his tail during the Battle of Britain.

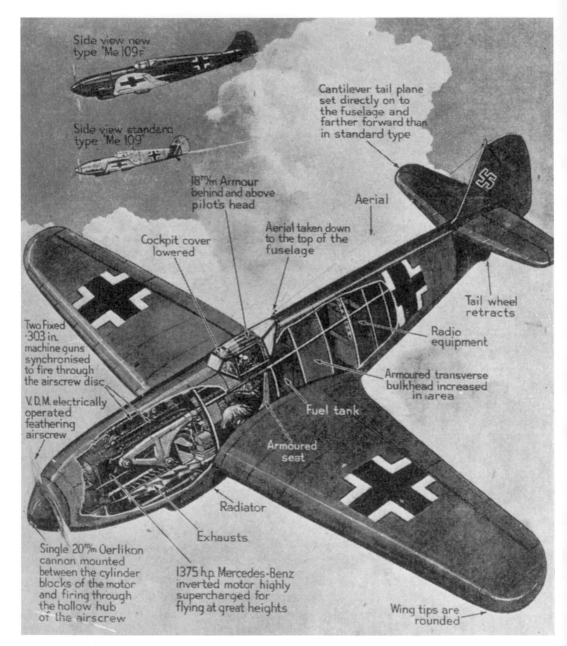

Side view new type 'Me 109 F'

Side view standard type 'Me 109'

Cantilever tail plane set directly on to the fuselage and farther forward than in standard type

18 m/m Armour behind and above pilot's head

Aerial

Aerial taken down to the top of the fuselage

Cockpit cover lowered

Tail wheel retracts

Radio equipment

Two Fixed ·303 in. machine guns synchronised to fire through the airscrew disc.

Armoured transverse bulkhead increased in area

V.D.M. electrically operated feathering airscrew

Fuel tank

Armoured seat

Radiator

Exhausts

Single 20 m/m Oerlikon cannon mounted between the cylinder blocks of the motor and firing through the hollow hub of the airscrew

1375 h.p. Mercedes-Benz inverted motor highly supercharged for flying at great heights

Wing tips are rounded

14

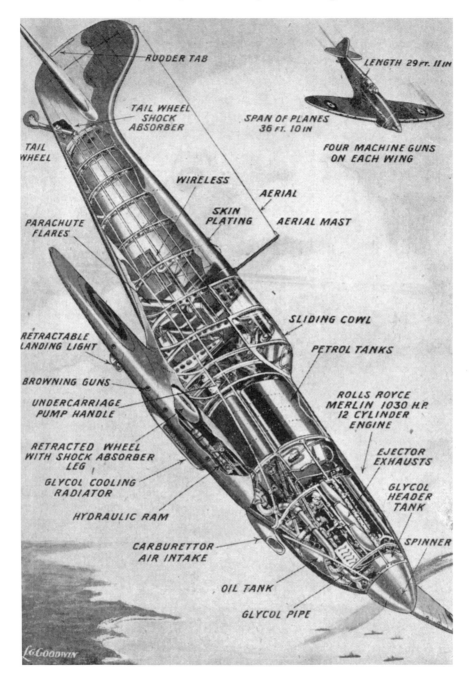

RUDDER TAB

TAIL WHEEL SHOCK ABSORBER

LENGTH 29 FT. 11 IN

SPAN OF PLANES 36 FT. 10 IN

TAIL WHEEL

FOUR MACHINE GUNS ON EACH WING

WIRELESS

PARACHUTE FLARES

SKIN PLATING

AERIAL

AERIAL MAST

SLIDING COWL

RETRACTABLE LANDING LIGHT

PETROL TANKS

BROWNING GUNS

ROLLS ROYCE MERLIN 1030 H.P. 12 CYLINDER ENGINE

UNDERCARRIAGE PUMP HANDLE

RETRACTED WHEEL WITH SHOCK ABSORBER LEG

EJECTOR EXHAUSTS

GLYCOL COOLING RADIATOR

GLYCOL HEADER TANK

HYDRAULIC RAM

SPINNER

CARBURETTOR AIR INTAKE

OIL TANK

GLYCOL PIPE

L.G.GOODWIN

15

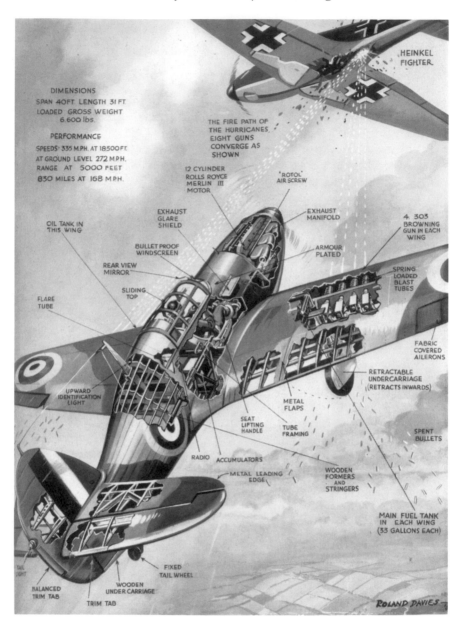

DIMENSIONS
SPAN 40FT LENGTH 31 FT.
LOADED GROSS WEIGHT
6.600 lbs.

PERFORMANCE
SPEEDS: 335 M.P.H. AT 18500 FT.
AT GROUND LEVEL 272 M.P.H.
RANGE AT 5000 FEET
830 MILES AT 168 M.P.H.

THE FIRE PATH OF
THE HURRICANES
EIGHT GUNS
CONVERGE AS
SHOWN

12 CYLINDER
ROLLS ROYCE
MERLIN III
MOTOR

'ROTOL'
AIR SCREW

EXHAUST
GLARE
SHIELD

EXHAUST
MANIFOLD

4. 303
BROWNING
GUN IN EACH
WING

OIL TANK IN
THIS WING

BULLET PROOF
WINDSCREEN

ARMOUR
PLATED

REAR VIEW
MIRROR

SPRING
LOADED
BLAST
TUBES

FLARE
TUBE

SLIDING
TOP

FABRIC
COVERED
AILERONS

RETRACTABLE
UNDERCARRIAGE
(RETRACTS INWARDS)

UPWARD
IDENTIFICATION
LIGHT

METAL
FLAPS

SEAT
LIFTING
HANDLE

TUBE
FRAMING

SPENT
BULLETS

RADIO   ACCUMULATORS

METAL LEADING
EDGE

WOODEN
FORMERS
AND
STRINGERS

MAIN FUEL TANK
IN EACH WING
(33 GALLONS EACH)

TAIL
LIGHT

FIXED
TAIL WHEEL

BALANCED
TRIM TAB

WOODEN
UNDER CARRIAGE

TRIM TAB

HEINKEL
FIGHTER

ROLAND DAVIES

A Spitfire readies for a night flight in 1940.

Hurricanes in formation over France in the winter of 1939/40.

Ready for the attack: Hurricanes gathered around a petrol bowser being refueled.

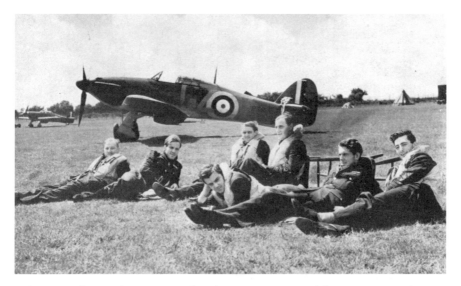

Taking a well-earned rest. RAF pilots having just returned from a sortie in the summer of 1940.

Douglas Bader (centre) during the Battle of Britain, with a Hurricane behind.

A Sergeant pilot shows how one button controls eight Browning machine guns in his Spitfire.

Test-firing a Spitfire's machine guns.

King George V inspects a Spitfire during the Battle of Britain.

Many Spitfires have reached preservation and, thanks to the Battle of Britain Memorial Flight, we can hear the sound of massed Merlin engines today at air shows and commemorations throughout the UK.

Two Spitfires shoot down a Heinkel He 111 during the Battle of Britain.

Many Messerschmitts were captured during the war. Here, one in RAF markings flies over England.

A Messerschmitt Bf 109 in RAF roundels in the North African desert.

A devil adorns this Messerschmitt about to be removed to the scrapheap and melted down to make more Spitfires.

This shot-down Messerschmitt Bf 109 is seen during a War Week in late 1940 in Sheffield.

A 109 on display in Paris before the fall of France.

Messerschmitts were sold to foreign air forces, including the Swiss. They were also made under licence in Spain and Czechoslovakia.

Opposite: A German propaganda photo of a Messerschmitt Bf 109 under maintenance during the Phoney War.

Spitfire

NOTES TO USERS

THIS publication is divided into five parts: Descriptive, Handling, Operating Data, Emergencies, and Illustrations. Part I gives only a brief description of the controls with which the pilot should be acquainted.

These Notes are complementary to A.P. 2095 Pilot's Notes General and assume a thorough knowledge of its contents. All pilots should be in possession of a copy of A.P. 2095 (see A.M.O. A93/43).

Words in capital letters indicate the actual markings on the controls concerned.

Additional copies may be obtained by the Station Publications Officer by application on Form 294A, in duplicate, to Command headquarters for onward transmission to A.P.F.S., 81 Fulham Road, S.W.3 (see A.M.O. A. 1114/44). The number of this publication must be quoted in full—A.P. 1565J, P & L —P.N.

Comments and suggestions should be forwarded through the usual channels to the Air Ministry (D.T.F.).

AIR MINISTRY   AIR PUBLICATION 1565J, P & L—P.N.
September 1946   *Pilot's Notes*
(*Reprinted—February* 1947)   *3rd Edition*

SPITFIRE IX, XI & XVI PILOT'S NOTES

3rd Edition. This Edition supersedes all previous issues.

LIST OF CONTENTS

PART I—DESCRIPTIVE

ENGINE CONTROLS   *Para.*

OTHER CONTROLS

PART II—HANDLING

PART III—OPERATING DATA *Para.*

PART IV—EMERGENCIES

PART V—ILLUSTRATIONS *Fig.*

AIR PUBLICATION 1565J, P & L—P.N.
Pilot's Notes

PART I

DESCRIPTIVE

NOTE.—The numbers quoted in brackets after items in
the text refer to key numbers of the illustrations
in Part V.

INTRODUCTION

1. (i) The variants of the Spitfire IX, XI and XVI are dis-
tinguished by prefix letters denoting the general operating
altitude or role and the suffix letter (e) is used where
·5-in. guns replace ·303-in. guns. The aircraft are all
essentially similar, but the following table shows the main
features that give the various versions their distinguishing
letters:

F IX	Merlin 61, 63 or 63A; two 20-mm. and four ·303-in. guns.
LF IX	Merlin 66; two 20-mm. and four ·303-in. guns.
LF IX (e)	Merlin 66; two 20-mm. and two ·5-in. guns.
HF IX	Merlin 70; two 20-mm. and four ·303-in. guns.
HF IX (e)	Merlin 70; two 20-mm. and two ·5-in. guns.
PR XI	Merlin 61, 63, 63A or 70.
F XVI	Merlin 266; two 20-mm. and two ·5-in. guns.

   (ii) Merlin 61 and 63 engines have S.U. float-type carburettors,
but on Merlin 66, 70 and 266 engines these are replaced
by Bendix-Stromberg injection carburettors.

   (iii) All these marks of aircraft are fitted with Rotol 4-bladed
hydraulic propellers and on the majority of the aircraft
the wing tips are clipped.

   (iv) Later Mk. IX and XVIs have "rear view" fuselages
which incorporate "tear-drop" sliding hoods.

PART I—DESCRIPTIVE

FUEL, OIL AND COOLANT SYSTEMS

2. **Fuel tanks** (see Fig. 4).—Fuel is carried in two tanks mounted one above the other (the lower one is self-sealing) forward of the cockpit. The top tank feeds into the bottom tank and fuel is delivered to the carburettor, through a filter, by an engine-driven pump. On Merlin 61 and 63 engine installations there is a fuel cooler, while on Bendix-Stromberg carburettor installations a de-aerator in the carburettor, for separating accumulated air from the fuel, is vented to the top tank. Later Mk. IX and all F. Mk. XVI aircraft mount two additional fuel tanks with a combined capacity of 75 gallons (66 gallons in aircraft with "rear view" fuselages); they are fitted in the fuselage behind the cockpit. These tanks should only be filled for special operations at the discretion of the appropriate Area Commander and normally their cocks should be wired OFF. If fitted in aircraft with "rear view" fuselages, they must not be used in any circumstances.

A.L.1
Part I
para. 2

The capacities of the main tanks are as follows :

Top tank	..	..	..	..	48 gallons
Bottom tank		..	..	..	37 gallons or 47* gallons
Total		..	..	..	85 gallons or 95* gallons

* On some aircraft; generally those with "rear-view" fuselages.

On PR XI aircraft there is a 66-gal. tank in each wing, bringing the total capacity up to 217 gal. These tanks feed the engine direct by gravity and the cocks are controlled by the two levers (red and green) fitted on the left-hand side below the rudder trim control. A contents gauge for the port tank is on the left-hand side and one for the starboard tank is high up on the right-hand side of the instrument panel.

An auxiliary "blister" drop tank of 30, 45 or 90-gal. capacity (on the PR XI, of 170 gal.) can be fitted under the fuselage; these tanks feed the engine direct and do not replenish the main tanks. To meet the possibility of engine cutting due to fuel boiling in warm weather at high altitudes, the main tanks are pressurised; pressurising, however, impairs the self-sealing properties of the tanks and should be turned OFF if a tank is holed.

3. **Fuel cocks.**—The cock control for the main tanks is a lever (47) fitted below the engine starting pushbuttons

PART I—DESCRIPTIVE

and the pressurising control (50) is below the right-hand side of the instrument panel. The cock control (58) and jettison lever (59) for the auxiliary drop tank are mounted together on the right-hand side of the cockpit, below the undercarriage control unit. The jettison lever is pulled up to jettison the drop tank, but cannot be operated until the cock control is moved forward to the OFF position. The cock for the rear fuselage tanks (when fitted) is to the left of the seat.

4. **Fuel pumps.**—On Bendix-Stromberg carburettor installations an electric booster pump, operated by a switch on the left-hand side of the cockpit, is fitted in the lower main tank. On early aircraft this pump is not fitted, but a hand wobble pump is provided instead, just forward of the remote contactor.

   NOTE.—On aircraft which have rear fuselage tanks a second pump is fitted (in the lower rear tank) and the control switch described above then has three positions.

5. **Fuel contents gauges and pressure warning light.**—The contents gauge (19) on the right-hand side of the instrument panel indicates the quantity of fuel in the lower main tank when the adjacent pushbutton is depressed. On aircraft with rear fuselage tanks a gauge (for the lower rear tank only) is mounted beside the main tanks' gauge. This also operates when the main tanks' gauge pushbutton is depressed. On later L.F. Mk. XVI aircraft the two gauges are mounted together, the left-hand dial (which is calibrated only up to 50 gallons) indicating the contents of the main tanks.

   The fuel pressure warning light (18) is operative when the switch (34) on the throttle quadrant is on and comes on at any time when fuel pressure at the carburettor falls appreciably below normal.

6. **Oil system.**—Oil is supplied by a tank of 7·5 gallons oil capacity under the engine mounting, which is pressurised to $2\frac{1}{2}$ lb./sq.in., and passes through a filter before entering the engine. An oil cooler is fitted in the underside

PART I—DESCRIPTIVE

of the port wing and oil pressure (20) and temperature (17) gauges are fitted on the instrument panel. When carrying an auxiliary drop tank of 170 gallons capacity a larger oil tank of either 8·5 or 14·5 gallons capacity must be fitted.

7. **Engine coolant system.**—On early aircraft only, circulation of the coolant through the underwing radiators is thermostatically controlled, the radiators being by-passed until the coolant reaches a certain temperature. The header tank is mounted above the reduction gear casing and is fitted with a relief valve. On all aircraft the radiator flaps are fully automatic and are designed to open at a coolant temperature of 115° C. A pushbutton is fitted on the electrical panel for ground testing, and there is a coolant temperature gauge (16) on the instrument panel.

8. **Intercooler system.**—On all aircraft the high temperatures resulting from two-stage supercharging necessitate the introduction of an intercooler between the supercharger delivery and the induction manifolds, particularly when S (high) gear is used. An auxiliary pump passes the coolant from a separate header tank to a radiator under the starboard wing, and thence through the supercharger casing to the intercooler, where the charge is cooled by loss of heat passing to the coolant. On early aircraft a thermostatically operated switch in the induction pipe is connected to the supercharger operating ram and causes it to change the supercharger to M (low) gear in the event of the charge temperature becoming excessive. This change of gear ratio is indicated to the pilot by a pushbutton, which springs out on the instrument panel. The supercharger will change back to high gear after the temperature of the charge has returned to normal and the pushbutton has been pushed in. If, however, the excessive temperature is of a permanent nature, due to failure of the intercooler system, the pushbutton will continue to spring out and the flight should be continued in low gear.

MAIN SERVICES

9. **Hydraulic system.**—Oil is carried in a reservoir on the fireproof bulkhead and passes through a filter to an engine-driven pump for operation of the undercarriage.

PART I—DESCRIPTIVE

10. **Electrical system.**—A 12-volt generator supplies an accumulator which in turn supplies the whole of the electrical installation. A voltmeter (10) across the accumulator is fitted at the top of the instrument panel and a red light (40), on the electrical panel, marked POWER FAILURE, is illuminated when the generator is not delivering current to the accumulator.

    NOTE.—If the electrical system fails or is damaged, the supercharger will be fixed in low gear and the radiator flaps will remain closed.

11. **Pneumatic system.**—An engine-driven air compressor charges two storage cylinders to a pressure of 300 lb./sq.in. for operation of the flaps, radiator flaps, supercharger ram, brakes and guns.

    NOTE.—If the pneumatic system fails, the supercharger will be fixed in low gear, but the position of the radiator flaps will depend on the nature of the failure.

AIRCRAFT CONTROLS

12. **Trimming tabs.**—The elevator trimming tabs are controlled by a handwheel (30) on the left-hand side of the cockpit, the indicator (24) being on the instrument panel. The rudder trimming tab is controlled by a small handwheel (27) and is not provided with an indicator. The aircraft tends to turn to starboard when the handwheel is rotated clockwise.

13. **Undercarriage control.**—The undercarriage selector lever (52) moves in a gated quadrant on the right-hand side of the cockpit.

    To raise the undercarriage the lever must be moved downwards and inwards to disengage it from the gate, and then moved forward smartly in one movement to the full extent of the quadrant. When the undercarriage is locked up the lever will automatically spring into the forward gate.

    To lower the undercarriage the lever must be held forward for about two seconds, then pulled back in one

PART I—DESCRIPTIVE

movement to the full extent of the quadrant. When the undercarriage is locked down the lever will spring into the rear gate.

Warning.—The lever must never be moved into either gate by hand as this will cut off the hydraulic pressure.

An indicator in the quadrant shows DOWN, IDLE or UP depending on the position of the hydraulic valve. UP and DOWN should show only during the corresponding operation of the undercarriage and IDLE when the lever is in either gate. If, when the engine is not running, the indicator shows DOWN, it should return to IDLE when the engine is started; if it does not, probable failure of the hydraulic pump is indicated.

14. **Undercarriage indicators**

(a) *Electrical visual indicator.*—The electrically operated visual indicator (2) has two semi-transparent windows on which the words UP on a red background and DOWN on a green background are lettered; the words are illuminated according to the position of the undercarriage. The switch (34) for the DOWN circuit is moved to the on position by a striker on the throttle lever as the throttle is opened.

(b) *Mechanical position indicators.*—On early aircraft a rod that extends through the top surface of the main plane is fitted to each undercarriage unit. When the wheels are down the rods protrude through the top of the main planes and when they are up, the tops of the rods, which are painted red, are flush with the main plane surfaces.

15. **Undercarriage warning horn.**—The horn, fitted in early aircraft only, sounds when the throttle lever is nearly closed and the undercarriage is not lowered. It cannot be silenced until the throttle is opened again or the undercarriage is lowered.

16. **Flaps control.**—The split flaps have two positions only, up and fully down. They are controlled by a finger lever (5) on the instrument panel.

PART I—DESCRIPTIVE

17. **Wheel brakes.**—The brake lever is fitted on the control column spade grip and a catch for retaining it in the on position for parking is fitted below the lever pivot. A triple pressure gauge (25), showing the air pressures in the pneumatic system cylinders and at each brake, is mounted on the instrument panel.

18. **Flying controls locking gear.**—Two struts are stowed on the right-hand side of the cockpit aft of the seat. The longer strut and the arm attached to it lock the control column to the seat and to the starboard datum longeron, and the shorter strut, attached to the other strut by a cable, locks the rudder pedals. The controls should be locked with the seat in its highest position.

ENGINE CONTROLS

19. **Throttle.**—The throttle lever (33) is gated at the climbing boost position. There is a friction adjuster (31) on the side of the quadrant. The mixture control is automatic and there is no pilot's control lever.

20. **Propeller control**

(i) On early aircraft the speed control lever (35) on the inboard side of the throttle quadrant varies the governed r.p.m. from 3,000 down to 1,800.

(ii) On later aircraft the propeller speed control is inter-connected with the throttle control. The inter-connection is effected by a lever, similar to the normal speed control lever, which is known as the override lever. When this is pulled back to the stop in the quadrant (the AUTO-MATIC position) the r.p.m. are controlled by the positioning of the throttle lever. When pushed fully forward to the MAX. R.P.M. position it overrides the interconnection device and r.p.m. are then governed at approximately 3,000. The override lever can be used in the same way as the conventional propeller speed control lever to enable the pilot to select higher r.p.m. than those given by the interconnection.

It must be remembered that the interconnection is effected only when the override lever is pulled back to

PART I—DESCRIPTIVE

the stop in the quadrant; indiscriminate use of the lever in any position forward of this stop will increase fuel consumption considerably.

At low altitudes (and at altitudes just above that at which high gear is automatically engaged) the corresponding r.p.m. for a given boost with the override lever set to AUTOMATIC are as follows:

Boost (lb./sq.in.)					*R.P.M.*
Below +3	..	..	..	..	1,800–1,850
At +7	..	..	..	..	2,270–2,370
At +12 (at the gate)	..	..	..	2,800–2,900
At +18 (throttle fully open)		..	..	3,000–3,050

(iii) A friction damping control (46) is fitted on the inboard side of the throttle quadrant.

21. **Supercharger controls.**—The two-speed two-stage supercharger automatically changes to high gear at about 21,000 feet (14,000 feet on Merlin 66 and 11,000 feet on Merlin 266 installations) on the climb and back to low gear at about 19,000 feet (12,500 feet on Merlin 66 and 10,000 feet on Merlin 266 installations) on the descent. An override switch is fitted on the instrument panel by means of which low gear may be selected at any height. There is a pushbutton (42) on the electrical panel for testing the gear change on the ground, and a red light (13) on the instrument panel comes on when high-gear is engaged, on the ground or in flight.

22. **Intercooler protector.**—See para. 8 and note. On early aircraft, should excessive charge temperatures cause the pushbutton (15) to spring out, it may be reset manually to allow the supercharger to return to high gear; it will, however, only remain in if the charge temperature has returned to normal.

23. **Radiator flap control.**—The radiator flaps are fully automatic and there is no manual control. A pushbutton (41) for testing the radiator flaps is on the electrical panel.

24. **Slow-running cut-out (Merlin 61 and 63 installations only).** —The control on the carburettor is operated by pulling the ring (37) below the left-hand side of the instrument panel.

PART I—DESCRIPTIVE

25. **Idle cut-off control (Merlin 66, 70 and 266 installations only).**—The idle cut-off valve on Bendix-Stromberg carburettors is operated by moving the short lever on the throttle quadrant through the gate to the fully aft position. On early Stromberg carburettor installations this lever is not fitted, but the cut-off valve is operated by the ring (37) which on other aircraft operates the slow-running cut-out.

   NOTE.—The idle cut-off control must be in the fully aft position, or cut-off position, at all times when a booster pump is on and the engine is not running; otherwise, fuel will be injected into the supercharger at high pressure and there will be, in consequence, a serious risk of fire.

26. **Carburettor air intake filter control**

   On tropicalised aircraft the carburettor air intake filter control on the left-hand side of the cockpit has two positions OPEN and CLOSED (NORMAL INTAKE and FILTER IN OPERATION on later aircraft). The CLOSED (or FILTER IN OPERATION) position must be used for all ground running, take-off and landing and when flying in sandy or dust-laden conditions.

   NOTE.— (i) In the air it may be necessary to reduce speed to 200 m.p.h. I.A.S. or less, before the filter control lever can be operated.

        (ii) The filter control lever must always be moved slowly.

27. **Cylinder priming pump.**—A hand-operated pump (48) for priming the engine is fitted below the right-hand side of the instrument panel.

28. **Ignition switches and starter buttons.**—The ignition switches (1) are on the left-hand side of the instrument panel and the booster-coil (22) and the engine starter (21) pushbuttons immediately below it. Each pushbutton is covered by a safety shield.

29. **Ground battery starting.**—The socket for starting from an external supply is mounted on the starboard engine bearer.

PART I—DESCRIPTIVE

OTHER CONTROLS

30. **Cockpit door.**—The cockpit door is fitted with a two-position catch which allows it to be partly opened, thus preventing the sliding hood from coming forward in the event of a crash or forced landing. It will be found that the catch operates more easily when the aircraft is airborne than when on the ground.

   NOTE.—On aircraft with "tear-drop" hoods, the two-position catch should not be used.

31. **Sliding hood controls**

   (i) On later Mk. IX and XVI aircraft the "tear-drop" hood is opened and closed by a crank handle mounted on the right-hand cockpit wall, above the undercarriage selector lever. The handle must be pulled inwards before it can be rotated. The hood may be locked in any intermediate position by releasing the crank handle which then engages with the locking ratchet.

   (ii) From outside the cockpit the hood may be opened and closed by hand provided the pushbutton below the starboard hood rail is held depressed.

   (iii) The hood may be jettisoned in emergency (see para. 59).

32. **Signal discharger.**—The recognition device fires one of six cartridges out of the top of the rear fuselage when the handle (39) to the left of the pilot's seat is pulled upwards. On some aircraft a pre-selector control (38) is mounted above the operating handle.

Air Publication 1565J, p & l—P.N.
Pilot's Notes

PART II

HANDLING

33. Management of the fuel system

Note.—Except for special operations as directed by the appropriate Area Commander, the rear fuselage tanks must not be used and their cocks should be wired OFF. On aircraft with " rear view " fuselages they must not be used.

(i) *Without a drop tank*

Start the engine, warm up, taxy and take-off on the main tanks; then, at 2,000 ft., change to the rear fuselage tanks (turning off the main tanks cock after the change has been made) and drain them; then revert to the main tanks.

(ii) *When fitted with a drop tank*

(a) *Without rear fuselage tanks:* Start the engine, warm up, taxy and take-off on the main tanks; then at 2,000 ft. turn ON the drop tank and turn OFF the main tanks cock. When the fuel pressure warning light comes on, or the engine cuts, turn OFF the drop tank cock and reselect the main tanks. (See Note (i) below.)

(b) *With rear fuselage tanks:* Start the engine, warm up, taxy and take-off on the main tanks; then, at 2,000 ft. change to the rear fuselage tanks and continue to use fuel from them until they contain only 30 gallons. Turn ON the drop tank (turning OFF the rear fuselage tanks cock when the change has been made) and drain it, then change back to the rear fuselage tanks and drain them. Revert to the main tanks.

Note.— (i) When it is essential to use all the fuel from the drop tank its cock must be turned OFF and the throttle closed immediately the engine cuts; a fresh tank should then be selected

PART II—HANDLING

without delay. The booster pump in the newly selected tank should be switched ON, or the hand wobble pump operated, to assist the engine to pick up but in addition to this it may be necessary to windmill the engine at high r.p.m. to ensure an adequate fuel supply.

(ii) Drop tanks should only be jettisoned if this is necessary operationally. If a drop tank is jettisoned before it is empty a fresh tank should be turned ON before the drop tank cock is turned OFF.

(iii) At no time must the drop tank cock and the rear fuselage tanks cock be on together or fuel from the rear fuselage tanks will drain into the drop tank since the connection from these tanks joins the drop tank connection below the non-return valve.

(iv) The drop tank cock must always be off when the tank has been jettisoned or is empty, otherwise air may be drawn into the main fuel system thus causing engine cutting.

(iii) *Use of the booster pump(s)*

(*a*) The main tanks booster pump should be switched ON for take-off and landing and at all times when these tanks are in use in flight.

(*b*) The rear fuselage tanks booster pump should be switched ON at all times when changing to, or using fuel from, these tanks.

34. Preliminaries

(i) Check that the undercarriage selector lever is down; switch on indicator and see that DOWN shows green.

(ii) Check the contents of the fuel tanks. If fitted with auxiliary tank(s) check that corresponding cock(s) are OFF.

(iii) Test the operation of the flying controls and adjust the rudder pedals for equal length.

PART II—HANDLING

(iv) On aircraft with Bendix-Stromberg carburettors ensure that the idle cut-off control is in the fully aft position, or cut-off position (see para. 25), then check the operation of the booster pump(s) by sound.

35. **Starting the engine and warming up** (Aircraft with Merlin 61 or 63 engines)

    (i) Set the fuel cock ..   ..   ON

(ii) Ignition switches	OFF
Throttle	½ in. – 1 in. open
Propeller speed control lever	Fully forward
Supercharger switch ..	AUTO. NORMAL POSITION
Carburettor air intake filter control	CLOSED or FILTER IN OPERATION (see para. 26)

(iii) If an external priming connection is fitted, high volatility fuel (Stores ref. 34A/III) should be used for priming at temperatures below freezing. Work the Ki-gass priming pump until the fuel reaches the priming nozzles; this may be judged by a sudden increase in resistance.

(iv) Switch ON the ignition and press the starter and booster-coil buttons. Turning periods must not exceed 20 seconds, with a 30 seconds wait between each. Work the priming pump as rapidly and vigorously as possible while the engine is being turned; it should start after the following number of strokes if cold:

Air temperature °C.	+30	+20	+10	0	−10	−20
Normal fuel	3	4	7	12	—	—
High volatility fuel	—	—	—	4	8	18

(v) At temperatures below freezing it will probably be necessary to continue priming after the engine has fired and until it picks up on the carburettor.

(vi) Release the starter button as soon as the engine starts, and as soon as the engine is running satisfactorily release the booster-coil button and screw down the priming pump.

(vii) Open up slowly to 1,000 to 1,200 r.p.m., then warm up at this speed.

PART II—HANDLING

36. Starting the engine and warming up (Aircraft with Merlin 66, 70 or 266 engines)

(i) Set the fuel cock   ON

(ii) Ignition switches .. ..   OFF
Throttle .. .. ..   ½ in. – 1 in. open
Propeller speed control (or override) lever .. .. Fully forward
Idle cut-off control .. .. Fully aft
Supercharger switch .. AUTO. NORMAL POSITION
Carburettor air intake filter control   CLOSED or FILTER IN OPERATION (see para. 26)

(iii) Switch ON the main tanks booster pump for 30 seconds (or operate the hand wobble pump for that period) then switch it OFF and set the idle cut-off control forward to the RUN position.

> NOTE.—If the idle cut-off control is operated by the ring described in para. 25, this must be held out (i.e., in the cut-off position) while the booster pump is ON or the hand wobble pump is being used.

(iv) An external priming connection is fitted and high volatility fuel (Stores Ref. 34A/111) should be used for priming at temperatures below freezing. Operate the priming pump until fuel reaches the priming nozzles (this may be judged by a sudden increase in resistance to the plunger) then prime the engine (if it is cold) with the following number of strokes

Air temperature °C.	+30	+20	+10	0	−10	−20
Normal fuel	3	4	7	12	—	—
High volatility fuel	—	—	—	4	8	18

(v) Switch ON the ignition and press the starter and booster-coil pushbuttons.

(vi) When the engine fires release the starter button; keep the booster-coil button depressed and operate the priming pump (if required) until the engine is running smoothly.

PART II—HANDLING

(vii) Screw down the priming pump then open up gradually to 1,000–1,200 r.p.m. and warm up at this speed.

(viii) Check that the fuel pressure warning light does not come on then switch ON the main tanks booster pump (if fitted).

37. **Testing the engine and services while warming up**

(i) Check all temperatures and pressures and the operation of the flaps.

(ii) Press the radiator flaps test pushbutton and have the ground crew check that the flaps open.

(iii) Test each magneto in turn as a precautionary check before increasing power further.

(iv) If a drop tank is carried check the flow of fuel from it by running on it for at least one minute.

After warming up to at least 15° C. (oil temperature) and 60° C. (coolant temperature),

(v) Open up to 0 lb./sq.in. boost and exercise and check the operation of the two-speed two-stage supercharger by pressing in and holding the test pushbutton. Boost should rise slightly and the red warning light should come on when high gear is engaged. Release the pushbutton after 30 seconds.

(vi) At the same boost, exercise (at least twice) and check the operation of the constant speed propeller by moving the speed control lever over its full governing range. Return the lever fully forward. Check that the generator is charging the accumulator by noting that the power failure warning light is out.

(vii) Test each magneto in turn; if the single ignition drop exceeds 150 r.p.m., the ignition should be checked at higher power—see sub. para. (ix) below.

NOTE.—*The following additional checks should be carried out after repair, inspection other than daily, when the single ignition drop at 0 lb./sq.in. boost exceeds 150 r.p.m., or at any time at the discretion of the pilot. When these checks are performed the tail of the aircraft must be securely lashed down.*

PART II—HANDLING

(viii) Open the throttle to the take-off setting and check boost and static r.p.m.

(ix) Throttle back until r.p.m. fall just below the take-off figure (thus ensuring that the propeller is not constant speeding) then test each magneto in turn. If the single ignition drop exceeds 150 r.p.m. the aircraft should not be flown.

(x) Where applicable (see para. 20) throttle back to +3 lb./sq.in. boost and set the override lever to AUTO-MATIC; r.p.m. should fall to 1,800-1,850. Return the lever to MAX. R.P.M.

(xi) Before taxying check the brake pressure (80 lb./sq.in.) and the pneumatic supply pressure (220 lb./sq.in.).

38. Check list before take-off

T—Trimming tabs

	At training load (full main tanks, no ammunition or external stores) 7,150 lb. (All Marks)	At normal full load (full main tanks, ammunition + 1 x 45-gallon "blister" drop tank) 7,800 lb. (Max. Mk. XI)	At max. load (full main and rear fuselage tanks, full ammunition, + 1 x 90-gallon "blister" drop tank) 8,700 lb. (IX & XVI)
Elevator	1 div. nose down	Neutral	1 div. nose down
Rudder	Fully right	Fully right	Fully right

P—Propeller control   Speed control (or override) lever fully forward

F—Fuel   ..   ..   Main tanks cock—ON
                       Drop tank cock—OFF
                       Rear fuselage tanks cock—OFF
                       Main tanks booster pump—ON

F—Flaps   ..   ..   UP

Supercharger   ..   Switch—AUTO-NORMAL POSITION
                       Red light out

Carburettor air   CLOSED or FILTER IN
intake filter control OPERATION (see para. 26)

PART II—HANDLING

39. Take-off

(i) At training and normal loads +7 lb./sq.in. to +9 lb./sq. in. boost is sufficient for take-off. After take-off, however, boost should be increased (where applicable) to +12lb./ sq.in. to minimise the possibility of lead fouling of the sparking plugs.

(ii) There is a tendency to swing to the left but this can easily be checked with the rudder.

(iii) When the rear fuselage tanks are full the aircraft pitches on becoming airborne and it is recommended that the undercarriage should not be retracted, nor the sliding hood closed, until a height of at least 100 feet has been reached.

(iv) After retracting the undercarriage it is essential to check that the red warning light comes on, since if the under-carriage fails to lock UP the airflow through the radiators and oil cooler will be much reduced and excessive tempera-tures will result.

NOTE.—It may be necessary to hold the undercarriage selector lever hard forward against the quadrant until the red warning light comes on.

(v) If interconnected throttle and propeller controls are fitted move the override lever smoothly back to AUTO-MATIC when comfortably airborne.

(vi) After take-off some directional retrimming will be necessary.

(vii) Unless operating in sandy or dust-laden conditions set the carburettor air intake filter control to OPEN (or NORMAL INTAKE) at 1,000 ft.

40. Climbing

At all loads the recommended climbing speed is 180 m.p.h. (155 kts) I.A.S. from sea level to operating height.

NOTE.— (i) With the supercharger switch at AUTO, high gear is engaged automatically when the aircraft reaches a predetermined height (see para. 21). This is the optimum height for the gear change if full combat power is being

PART II—HANDLING

used, but if normal climbing power (2,850 r.p.m. + 12 lb./sq.in. boost) is being used the maximum rate of climb is obtained by delaying the gear change until the boost in low gear has fallen to + 8 lb./sq.in.

This is achieved by leaving the supercharger switch at MS until the boost has fallen to this figure.

(ii) Use of the air intake filter reduces the full throttle height considerably.

41. General flying

(i) *Stability*

(*a*) At light load (no fuel in the rear fuselage tanks, no drop tank) stability about all axes is satisfactory and the aircraft is easy and pleasant to fly.

(*b*) When the rear fuselage tanks are full there is a very marked reduction in longitudinal stability, the aircraft tightens in turns at all altitudes and, in this condition, is restricted to straight flying, and only gentle manœuvres; accurate trimming is not possible and instrument flying should be avoided whenever possible.

(*c*) When a 90-gallon drop tank is carried in addition to full fuel in the rear fuselage tanks the aircraft becomes extremely difficult and tiring to fly and in this condition is restricted to straight flying and only gentle manœuvres at low altitudes.

(*d*) On aircraft which have " rear view " fuselages there is a reduction in directional stability so that the application of yaw promotes marked changes of lateral and longitudinal trim. This characteristic is more pronounced at high altitudes.

(*e*) When 90 (or 170) gallon drop tanks are carried on these aircraft, they are restricted to straight flying and gentle manœuvres only.

(ii) *Controls*

The elevator and rudder trimming tabs are powerful and sensitive and must always be used with care, particularly at high speed.

PART II—HANDLING

(iii) *Changes of trim*

Undercarriage up ..	Nose up
Undercarriage down	Nose down
Flaps up	Nose up
Flaps down	Strongly nose down

There are marked changes of directional trim with change of power and speed. These should be countered by accurate use of the rudder trimming tab control.

The firing of salvos of R/P's promotes a nose-up change of trim; this change of trim is most marked when the weapons are fired in level flight at about 300 m.p.h. (258 kts) I.A.S.

(iv) *Flying at reduced airspeed in conditions of poor visibility.* Reduce speed to 160 m.p.h. (140 kts) I.A.S., lower the flaps and set the propeller speed control (or override) lever to give 2,650 r.p.m.; open the sliding hood. Speed may then be reduced to 140 m.p.h. (120 kts) I.A.S.

42. Stalling

(i) The stalling speeds, engine " off ", in m.p.h. (knots) I.A.S. are

Aircraft without "rear-view" fuselages

	At training load (full main tanks, no ammunition or external stores) 7,150 lb.	At normal full load (full main tanks, full ammunition + 1 × 45-gallon "blister" drop tank) 7,800 lb.	At maximum load (full main and rear fuselage tanks, full ammunition + 1 × 90-gallon "blister" drop tank) 8,700 lb.
Undercarriage and flaps up ..	90 (78)	93 (80)	100 (86)
Undercarriage and flaps down	75–79(65–69)	80 (69)	84 (72)

Aircraft with "rear view" fuselages

Undercarriage and flaps up	95 (83)	98 (85)	115–117 (100–102)
Undercarriage and flaps down	82–84 (71–73)	85 (98)	95 (83)

The speeds above apply to aircraft which have " clipped " wings. On aircraft with " full span " wings these speeds are reduced (at all loads by some 3–6 m.p.h. (or kts) I.A.S.

PART II—HANDLING

(ii) Warning of the approach of a stall is given by tail buffeting, the onset of which can be felt some 10 m.p.h. (9 kts) I.A.S. before the stall itself. At the stall either wing and the nose drop gently. Recovery is straightforward and easy.

If the control column is held back at the stall tail buffeting becomes very pronounced and the wing drop is more marked.

NOTE.—On L.F. Mk. XVI aircraft warning of the approach of a stall is not so clear; faint tail buffeting can be felt some 5 m.p.h. (or kts) I.A.S. before the stall occurs.

(iii) When the rear fuselage tanks are full there is an increasing tendency for the nose to rise as the stall is approached. This self-stalling tendency must be checked by firm forward movement of the control column.

(iv) Warning of the approach of a stall in a steep turn is given by pronounced tail buffeting (and on F. Mk. XVI aircraft by hood rattling). If the acceleration is then increased the aircraft will, in general, flick out of the turn.

43. Spinning

(i) Spinning is permitted, but the loss of height involved in recovery may be very great and the following limits are to be observed:

(*a*) Spins are not to be started below 10,000 feet.

(*b*) Recovery must be initiated before two turns are completed.

(ii) A speed of 180 m.p.h. (156 kts) I.A.S. should be attained before starting to ease out of the resultant dive.

(iii) Spinning is not permitted when fitted with a drop tank, when carrying a bomb load, or with any fuel in the rear fuselage tank.

44. Diving

(i) At training loads the aircraft becomes increasingly tail heavy as speed is gained and should, therefore, be trimmed into the dive. The tendency to yaw to the right should be corrected by accurate use of the rudder trimming tab control.

PART II—HANDLING

(ii) When carrying wing bombs the angle of dive must not exceed 60°; when carrying a fuselage bomb the angle of dive must not exceed 40°.

NOTE.—Until the rear fuselage tanks contain less than 30 gallons of fuel the aircraft is restricted to straight flight and only gentle manœuvres.

45. Aerobatics

(i) Aerobatics are not permitted when carrying any external stores (except the 30-gallon " blister " drop tank) nor when the rear fuselage tanks contain more than 30 gallons of fuel, *and are not recommended when the rear fuselage tanks contain any fuel.*

(ii) The following minimum speeds in m.p.h. (knots) I.A.S. are recommended:

Loop	300 (260)
Roll	240 (206)
Half-roll off loop ..	3;0 (295)
Climbing roll ..	330 (286)

(iii) Flick manoeuvres are not permitted.

46. Check list before landing

(i) Reduce speed to 160 m.p.h. (138 kts) I.A.S., open the sliding hood and check:

U—Undercarriage	DOWN
P—Propeller control ..	Speed control (or override) lever set to give 2,650 r.p.m.—fully forward on the final approach
Supercharger	Red light out
Carburettor air intake filter control	CLOSED (or FILTER IN OPERATION)—see para. 26.
F—Fuel	Main tanks cock ON
.	Main tanks booster pump (if fitted)—ON
F—Flaps	DOWN

(ii) Check brake pressure (80 lb./sq.in.) and pneumatic supply pressure (220 lb./sq.in.).

NOTE.—The rate of undercarriage lowering is much reduced at low r.p.m.

PART II—HANDLING

47. Approach and landing

(i) The recommended final approach speeds* in m.p.h. (kts) I.A.S. are

At training load (full main tanks, no ammunition or external stores) 7,150 lb.

(*a*) Aircraft without " rear-view " fuselages

	Engine assisted	Glide
Flaps down	95 (82)	105 (90)
Flaps up	105 (90)	110 (95)

(*b*) Aircraft with " rear-view " fuselages

	Engine assisted	Glide
Flaps down	100–105 (86–90)	115–120 (100–104)
Flaps up	115 (100)	120–125 (104–108)

*These are the speeds at which the airfield boundary is crossed; the initial straight approach should, however, be made at a speed 20–25 m.p.h. (17–21 kts) I.A.S. above these figures.

NOTE.—The speeds above apply to aircraft which have " clipped " wings; on aircraft with " full span " wings they may be safely reduced by 5 m.p.h. (or kts) I.A.S.

(ii) Should it be necessary in emergency to land with the rear fuselage tanks still containing all their fuel the final engine-assisted approach speeds given in (i) above should be increased by 10–15 m.p.h. (9–13 kts) I.A.S. The tendency for the nose to rise of its own accord at the " hold-off " must be watched (see para. 42 (iii)); the throttle should be closed only when contact with the ground is made.

(iii) The aircraft is nose-heavy on the ground; the brakes, therefore, must be used carefully on landing.

48. Mislanding

(i) At normal loads the aircraft will climb away easily with the undercarriage and flaps down and the use of full take-off power is unnecessary.

PART II—HANDLING

(ii) Open the throttle steadily to give the required boost.

(iii) Retract the undercarriage immediately.

(iv) With the flaps down climb at about 140 m.p.h. I.A.S.

(v) Raise the flaps at 300 ft. and retrim.

49. Beam approach

SPITFIRE Mk. XVI, at "training" load	Preliminary Approach	Inner Marker on Q.D.R.	Outer Marker on Q.D.R.	Inner Marker on Q.D.M.
Indicated height (ft.)	Down to 1,000	1,000	700–800	150
Action	—	Lower the under-carriage†	Lower the flaps	Throttle back slowly
Resultant change of trim	—	Nose down	Nose down	Slightly nose down
I.A.S. m.p.h. (knots)	170 (146)	160 (138)	130 (112)	110 (95)
R.P.M.	2,650	2,650	3,000*	3,000*
Boost (level flight)	−2	−2	−3	
Boost (−500 ft./min.)	−3	−3	−4	
Boost (overshoot)	—	—	—	+7

Remarks

† Reduce speed to 160 m.p.h. (138 kts) I.A.S. before lowering the under-carriage.

* With the override lever at MAX. R.P.M., r.p.m. may be 3,000–3,050 (see para. 20)

Altimeter error at take-off −50 ft.
Altimeter error at touchdown −60 ft.
Add 2 mbs. to Q.F.E. to give zero reading at touchdown.

OVERSHOOT
Open the throttle to give +7 lb./sq.in. boost. Raise the undercarriage and climb at 130 m.p.h. (112 kts) I.A.S. Raise the flaps at 300 ft. and retrim.

PART II—HANDLING

50. **After landing**

(i) *Before taxying*

Raise the flaps and switch OFF the main tanks booster pump (if fitted).

(ii) *On reaching dispersal*

(*a*) Open up to o lb./sq.in. boost and exercise the two-speed two-stage supercharger once (see para. 35 (v)).

(*b*) Throttle back slowly to 800–900 r.p.m. and idle at this speed for a few seconds then stop the engine by operating the slow running cut-out or idle cut-off control.

(*c*) When the propeller has stopped rotating switch OFF the ignition and all other electrical services.

(*d*) Turn OFF the fuel.

(iii) *Oil dilution (see A.P. 2095)*

The correct dilution periods are

At air temperatures above −10° C.   ..   1 minute.
At air temperatures below −10° C.   ..   2 minutes.

Air Publication 1565J, p & l—P.N.
Pilot's Notes

PART III

OPERATING DATA

51. Engine data : Merlins 61, 63, 66, 70 and 266

(i) Fuel—100 octane only.

(ii) Oil—See A.P. 1464/C.37.

(iii) The principal engine limitations are as follows :

	Sup.	R.p.m.	Boost	Temp. ° C. Coolant	Oil
MAX. TAKE-OFF TO 1,000 FT.	M	3,000†	+18*	135	—
MAX. CLIMBING 1 HOUR LIMIT	M S	2,850	+12	125	90
MAXIMUM CONTINUOUS	M S	2,650	+ 7	105 (115)	90
COMBAT 5 MINS. LIMIT	M S	3,000	+18‡	135	105

The figure in brackets is permissible for short periods.

† With interconnected controls there is a tolerance on "maximum" r.p.m.—see para. 20.

* +12 lb./sq.in. on Merlin 61 and 63 engines.

‡ +15 lb./sq.in. on Merlin 61 engine.

OIL PRESSURE:
   MINIMUM IN FLIGHT .. .. .. 30 lb./sq.in.

MINIMUM TEMP. °C. FOR TAKE-OFF:
   COOLANT .. .. 60° C.
   OIL .. .. 15° C.

PART III—OPERATING DATA

52. Flying limitations

(i) *Maximum speeds in m.p.h. (knots) I.A.S.*

Diving (without external stores), corresponding to a Mach.
No. of ·85:

Between S.L. and 20,000 ft.	—450 (385)
20,000 & 25,000 ft.	—430 (370)
25,000 & 30,000 ft.	—390 (335)
30,000 & 35,000 ft.	—340 (292)
Above 35,000 ft.	—310 (265)
Undercarriage down	—160 (138)
Flaps down	—160 (138)

Diving (with the following external stores):

(a) With 1 × 500 lb. AN/M 58 bomb,
    or 1 × 500 lb. AN/M 64 bomb,
    or 1 × 500 lb. AN/M 76 bomb,
    or 1 × 65 nickel bomb Mk. II

        Below 20,000 ft.*—440 (378)

(b) With 1 × 500 lb. S.A.P. bomb
    or Smoke bomb Mk. II

        Below 25,000 ft.*—400 (344)

(c) With 10 lb. practice bomb

        Below 25,000 ft.*—420 (360)

*Above these heights the limitations for the " clean "
aircraft apply.

(ii) *Maximum weights in lbs.*

For take-off and gentle
  manœuvres only .. .. Mks. IX & XVI—8,700*
For landing (except in
  emergency) .. .. Mks. IX & XVI—7,450
For take-off, all forms of
  flying and landing .. Mk. XI —7,800

*At this weight take-off must be made only from a smooth
hard runway.

(iii) *Flying restrictions*

(a) Rear fuselage tanks may be used only with special
authority and never on aircraft with " rear view " fuselages.

PART III—OPERATING DATA

(*b*) Aerobatics and combat manœuvres are not permitted when carrying any external stores (except the 30-gallon " blister " type drop tank) nor when the rear fuselage tanks contain more than 30 gallons of fuel (but see para. 45).

(*c*) When a 90 (or 170) gallon drop tank or a bomb load is carried the aircraft is restricted to straight flying and only gentle manœuvres.

(*d*) When wing bombs are carried in addition to a drop tank or fuselage bomb, take-off must be made only from a smooth hard runway.

(*e*) When carried, the 90 (or 170) gallon drop tank must be jettisoned before any dive bombing is commenced.

(*f*) The angle of dive when releasing a bomb or bomb load must not exceed 60° for wing bombs or 40° for a fuselage bomb.

(*g*) Except in emergency the fuselage bomb or drop tank must be jettisoned before landing with wing bombs fitted.

(*h*) Drop tanks should not be jettisoned unless necessary operationally. While jettisoning, the aircraft should be flown straight and level at a speed not greater than 300 m.p.h. I.A.S.

(*i*) Except in emergency landings should not be attempted until the rear fuselage tanks contain less than 30 gallons of fuel. Should a landing be necessary when they contain a greater quantity of fuel the drop tank (if fitted) should be jettisoned.

53. Position error corrections

From	120	150	170	210	240	290	} m.p.h.
To	150	170	210	240	290	350	} I.A.S.
Add	4	2	0				} m.p.h.
Subtract			0	2	4	6	} or kts.
From	106	130	147	180	208	250	} Knots
To	130	147	180	208	250	300	} I.A.S.

PART III—OPERATING DATA

54. Maximum performance

(i) *Climbing*

(*a*) The speeds in m.p.h. (knots) for maximum rate of climb are

Sea level to 26,000 ft. —160 (140) I.A.S.
26,000 ft. to 30,000 ft. —150 (130)   ,,
30,000 ft. to 33,000 ft. —140 (122)   ,,
33,000 ft. to 37,000 ft. —130 (112)   ,,
37,000 ft. to 40,000 ft. —120 (104)   ,,
Above 40,000 ft.   —110 (95)   ,,

(*b*) With the supercharger switch at AUTO, high gear is engaged automatically when the aircraft reaches a pre-determined height (see para. 21). This is the optimum height for the gear change if full combat power is being used, but if normal climbing power (2,850 r.p.m. + 12 lb./sq.in. boost) is being used the maximum rate of climb is obtained by delaying the gear change until the boost in low gear has fallen to +8 lb./sq.in.

This is achieved by leaving the supercharger switch at MS until the boost has fallen to this figure.

(ii) *Combat*

Set the supercharger switch to AUTO and open the throttle fully.

NOTE.—On those aircraft which do not have interconnected throttle and propeller controls the propeller speed control lever must be advanced to the maximum r.p.m. position before the throttle is opened fully.

55. Economical flying

(i) *Climbing*

On aircraft not fitted with interconnected throttle and propeller controls.

(*a*) Set the supercharger switch to MS, the propeller speed control lever to give 2,650 r.p.m. and climb at the

PART III—OPERATING DATA

speeds given in para. 54 (i), opening the throttle progressively to maintain a boost pressure of +7 lb./sq.in.

(*b*) Set the supercharger switch to AUTO when the maximum obtainable boost in low gear is +3 lb./sq.in., throttling back to prevent overboosting as the change to high gear is made.

On aircraft fitted with interconnected throttle and propeller controls

(*a*) Set the supercharger switch to MS, set the throttle to give +7 lb./sq.in. boost and climb at the speeds given in para. 54 (i).

(*b*) As height is gained the boost will fall and it will be necessary to advance the throttle progressively to restore it. The throttle must not, however, be advanced beyond a position at which r.p.m. rise to 2,650. Set the supercharger switch to AUTO when, at this throttle setting, the boost in low gear has fallen to +3 lb./sq.in.

NOTE.—Climbing at the speeds given in para. 54 (i) will ensure greatest range, but for ease of control (especially at heavy loads and with the rear fuselage tanks full of fuel) a climbing speed of 180 m.p.h. (155 kts) I.A.S. from sea level to operating height is recommended. The loss of range will be only slight.

(ii) *Cruising*

The recommended speed for maximum range is 170 m.p.h. (147 kts) I.A.S. if the aircraft is lightly loaded. At heavy loads, especially if the rear fuselage tanks are full this speed can be increased to 200 m.p.h. (172 kts) I.A.S. without incurring a serious loss of range.

PART III—OPERATING DATA

On aircraft not fitted with interconnected throttle and propeller controls

(*a*) With the supercharger switch at MS fly at the maximum obtainable boost (not exceeding + 7 lb./sq.in.) and obtain the recommended speed by reducing r.p.m. as required.

NOTE.— (i) R.p.m. should not be reduced below a minimum of 1,800. At low altitudes, therefore, it may be necessary to reduce boost or the recommended speed will be exceeded.

(ii) As the boost falls at high altitudes it will not be possible to maintain the recommended speed in low gear, even at maximum continuous r.p.m. and full throttle. It will then be necessary to set the supercharger switch to AUTO. Boost will thus be restored and it will be possible to reduce r.p.m. again (as outlined in (*a*) above).

(iii) In both low and high gears r.p.m. which promote rough running should be avoided.

On aircraft fitted with interconnected throttle and propeller controls

Set the supercharger switch to MS and adjust the throttle to obtain the recommended speed. Avoid a throttle setting which promotes rough running.

NOTE.—At moderate and high altitudes it will be necessary to advance the throttle progressively to restore the falling boost and thus maintain the recommended speed.

Now as the throttle is opened r.p.m. will increase and at a certain height the recommended speed will be unobtainable even at a throttle setting which gives 2,650 r.p.m. At this height the supercharger switch should be set to AUTO and the throttle then adjusted as before to maintain the recommended speed.

PART III—OPERATING DATA

56. Fuel capacities and consumption

(i) *Normal fuel capacity:*

Top tank	..	..	..	..	.. 48 gallons
Bottom tank	..	..	..	..	.. 37 gallons
Total ..	..	..	..	..	.. 85 gallons

(ii) *Long-range fuel capacities:*

With 30-gallon " blister " drop tank..	.. 115 gallons
With 45-gallon " blister " drop tank..	.. 130 gallons
With 90-gallon " blister " drop tank..	.. 175 gallons
With 170-gallon " blister " drop tank	.. 255 gallons
With rear fuselage tanks	
Early aircraft .. .. · ..	.. 160 gallons
Later aircraft	.. 151 gallons

NOTE.—On some aircraft these capacities are increased by 10 gallons.

(iii) *Fuel consumptions:*

The approximate fuel consumptions (gals./hr.) are as follows:

Weak mixture (as obtained at +7 lb./sq.in. boost and below):

Boost lb./sq.in.	R.p.m.				
	2,650	2,400	2,200	2,000	1,800
+7	80	—	—	—	—
+4	71	66	61	54	—
+2	66	61	57	50	43
0	60	55	51	45	39
−2	53	49	45	40	35
−4	45	42	38	34	30

PART III—OPERATING DATA

Rich mixture (as obtained above + 7 lb./sq.in. boost):

Boost lb./sq.in.	R.p.m.	gals./hr.
+15	3,000	130
+12	2,850	105

NOTE.—The above approximate consumptions apply for all Marks of engine. Accurate figures giving the variation in consumption with height and as between low and high gear are not available.

AIR PUBLICATION 1565J, P & L—P.N.
Pilot's Notes

PART IV

EMERGENCIES

57. Undercarriage emergency operation

(i) If the selector lever jams and cannot be moved to the fully down position after moving it out of the gate, return it to the fully forward position for a few seconds to take the weight of the wheels off the locking pins and allow them to turn freely, then move it to the DOWN position.

(ii) If, however, the lever is jammed so that it cannot be moved either forward or downward, it can be released by taking the weight of the wheels off the locking pins either by pushing the control column forward sharply or inverting the aircraft. The lever can then be moved to the DOWN position.

(iii) If the lever springs into the gate and the indicator shows that the undercarriage is not locked down, hold it fully down for a few seconds. If this is not successful, raise and then lower the undercarriage again.

(iv) If the undercarriage still does not lock down, ensure that the lever is in the DOWN position (this is essential) and push the emergency lever forward and downward through 180°.

> NOTE.—(*a*) The emergency lever must not be returned to its original position and no attempt must be made to raise the undercarriage until the CO_2 cylinder has been replaced.
>
> (*b*) If the CO_2 cylinder has been accidentally discharged with the selector lever in the up position, the undercarriage will not lower unless the pipeline from the cylinder is broken, either by hand or by means of the crowbar.

PART IV—EMERGENCIES

58. Failure of the pneumatic system

(i) If the flaps fail to lower when the control is moved to the DOWN position, it is probably due to a leak in the pipeline, resulting in complete loss of air pressure and consequent brake failure.

(ii) Alternatively, if a leak develops in the flaps control system the flaps will lower, but complete loss of air pressure will follow and the brakes will become inoperative. (In this case a hissing sound may be heard in the cockpit after selecting flaps DOWN.)

(iii) In either case the flaps control should immediately be returned to the UP position in order to allow sufficient pressure to build up, so that a landing can be made with the brakes operative but without flaps.

> NOTE.—As a safeguard pilots should always check the pneumatic pressure supply after selecting flaps DOWN.

59. Hood jettisoning

The hood may be jettisoned in an emergency by pulling the rubber knob inside the top of the hood forward and downward and then pushing the lower edge of the hood outwards with the elbows.

> WARNING.—Before jettisoning the hood the seat should be lowered and the head then kept well down.

60. Forced landing

In the event of engine failure necessitating a forced landing:

(i) If a drop tank or bomb load is carried it should be jettisoned.

(ii) The fuel cut-off control (if fitted) should be pulled fully back.

(iii) The booster pump (if fitted) should be switched OFF.

PART IV—EMERGENCIES

(iv) The sliding hood should be opened and the cockpit door set on the catch (see para. 31).

(v) A speed of at least 150 m.p.h. (130 kts) I.A.S. should be maintained while manœuvring with the undercarriage and flaps retracted.

(vi) The flaps must not be lowered until it is certain that the selected landing area is within easy gliding reach.

(vii) The final straight approach should be made at the speeds given in para. 47.

(viii) If oil pressure is still available the glide can be lengthened considerably by pulling the propeller speed control (or override) lever fully back past the stop in the quadrant.

61. Ditching

(i) Whenever possible the aircraft should be abandoned by parachute rather than ditched, since the ditching qualities are known to be very poor.

(ii) When ditching is inevitable any external stores should be jettisoned (release will be more certain if the aircraft is gliding straight) and the following procedure observed:

(a) The cockpit hood should be jettisoned.

(b) The flaps should be lowered in order to reduce the touchdown speed as much as possible.

(c) The undercarriage should be kept retracted.

(d) The safety harness should be kept tightly adjusted and the R/T plug should be disconnected.

(e) The engine, if available, should be used to help make the touchdown in a taildown attitude at as low a forward speed as possible.

PART IV—EMERGENCIES

(*f*) Ditching should be along the swell, or into wind if the swell is not steep, but the pilot should be prepared for a tendency for the aircraft to dive when contact with the water is made.

62. Crowbar

A crowbar for use in emergency is stowed in spring clips on the cockpit door.

PART V—*ILLUSTRATIONS*

KEY to Figs. 1, 2 and 3

1. Ignition switches.
2. Undercarriage indicator.
3. Oxygen regulator.
4. Navigation lamps switch.
5. Flap control.
6. Instrument flying panel.
7. Lifting ring for sunscreen.
8. Reflector sight switch.
9. Reflector sight base.
10. Voltmeter.
11. Cockpit ventilator control.
12. Engine-speed indicator.
13. Supercharger warning lamp.
14. Boost gauge.
15. Intercooler protector pushbutton.
16. Coolant temperature gauge.
17. Oil temperature gauge.
18. Fuel pressure warning lamp.
19. Fuel contents gauge and pushbutton.
20. Oil pressure gauge.
21. Engine starter pushbutton.
22. Booster-coil pushbutton.
23. Cockpit floodlight switches.
24. Elevator tab position indicator.
25. Brake triple pressure gauge.
26. Crowbar.
27. Rudder trimming tab handwheel.
28. Pressure-head heater switch.
29. Two-position door catch lever.
30. Elevator trimming tab handwheel.
31. Throttle lever friction adjuster.
32. Floodlight.
33. Throttle lever.
34. Undercarriage indicator master switch.
35. Propeller speed control.
36. T.R.1133 pushbutton control.
37. Slow-running cut-out.
38. Signal discharger pre-selector control.
39. Signal discharger firing control.
40. Power failure lamp.
41. Radiator ground test pushbutton.
42. Supercharger ground test pushbutton.
43. Oil dilution pushbutton.
44. Map case.
45. Rudder pedal adjusting starwheel.
46. Propeller control friction adjuster.
47. Fuel cock control.
48. Engine priming pump.
49. Signalling switchbox.
50. Fuel tank pressure cock.
51. Remote contactor and contactor switch.
52. Undercarriage control lever.
53. IFF pushbuttons.
54. Harness release control.
55. IFF master switch.
56. Undercarriage emergency lowering control.
57. Rudder pedal adjusting starwheel.
58. Drop tank cock control.
59. Drop tank jettison lever.
60. Windscreen de-icing cock.
61. Seat adjustment lever.
62. Windscreen de-icing needle valve.
63. Windscreen de-icing pump.
64. Microphone/telephone socket.
65. Oxygen supply cock.

INSTRUMENT PANEL

FIG. 1

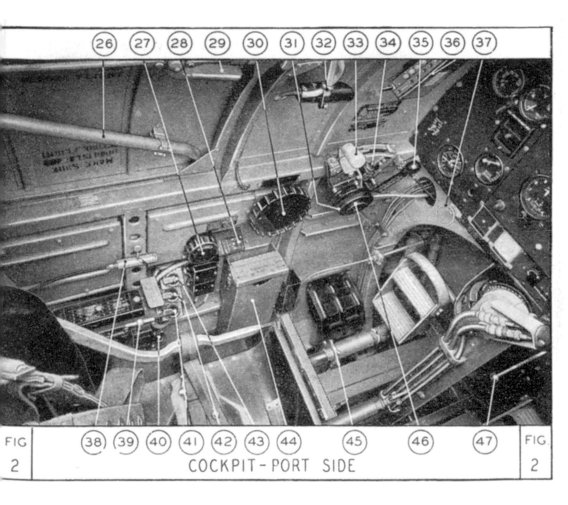

FIG 2

COCKPIT – PORT SIDE

FIG 2

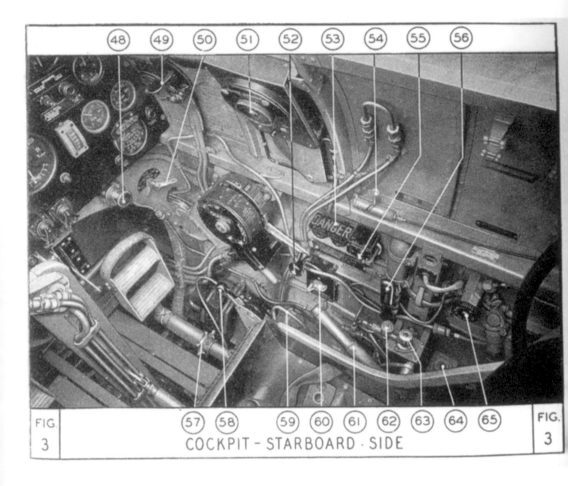

FIG. 3

COCKPIT - STARBOARD · SIDE

FIG. 3

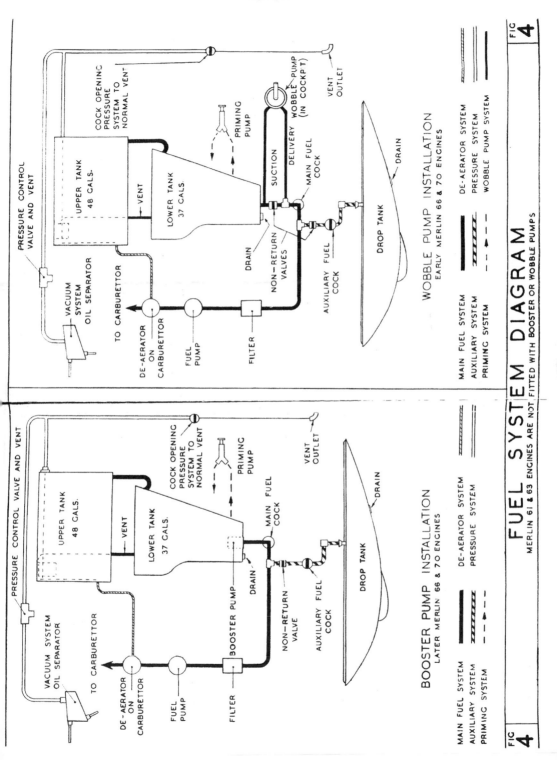

WOBBLE PUMP INSTALLATION
EARLY MERLIN 66 & 70 ENGINES

MAIN FUEL SYSTEM	DE-AERATOR SYSTEM
AUXILIARY SYSTEM	PRESSURE SYSTEM
PRIMING SYSTEM	WOBBLE PUMP SYSTEM

BOOSTER PUMP INSTALLATION
LATER MERLIN 66 & 70 ENGINES

MAIN FUEL SYSTEM	DE-AERATOR SYSTEM
AUXILIARY SYSTEM	PRESSURE SYSTEM
PRIMING SYSTEM	

FUEL SYSTEM DIAGRAM

MERLIN 61 & 63 ENGINES ARE NOT FITTED WITH BOOSTER OR WOBBLE PUMPS

FIG 4

Messerschmitt Bf 109E

Scope of Investigation

The handling tests conducted on the Bf 109 covered the following areas: take off and landing; trim and stability; 'one control' tests, flat turns and sideslips; stalling tests; high speed dive and 'feel' of the aircraft's controls.

Performance of the Aircraft

The weight of the aircraft during these tests was 5,600 lb, there is an error factor of 2–3% for the speeds quoted.

Top Level Speed:
At 16,400 ft – 355 mph, 2,400 rpm +2.3 lb/square inch boost pressure with radiators closed.
At 14,800 ft – 330 mph, 2,400 rpm +2.1 lb/sq. in. boost pressure with radiators open.

Rate of Climb to Height

Height (ft)	RPM	Boost lb/sq. in.	Rate of Climb Ft/min	Measured time to height
3,280	2,430	+3.9	2,740	1 min – 16 sec
6,560	2,430	+3.7	2,530	2 min – 31 sec
9,850	2,430	+3.6	2,900	3 min – 50 sec
13,150	2,430	+3.5	2,990	5 min – 03 sec
16,450	2,430	+2.0	2,600	6 min – 20 sec
19,750	2,400	+0.2	1,860	8 min - 01 sec
23,000	2,400	-1.8	1,450	10 min - 02 sec
26,300	2,400	-3.6	820	13 min – 35 sec

Absolute ceiling - 32,000 ft

General Description

The Bf 109 is a low wing monoplane of clean design. The construction is all-metal except for the moveable control surfaces and flaps which are fabric covered. The standard of surface finishing is high, all the metal coverings being flush riveted. The design allows for easy maintenance and all parts can be readily removed and replaced. The all up weight of the aircraft is 5,600 lb.

Engine

The engine fitted is a Daimler-Benz DB 601. The engine consists of a 12 cylinder, 60° inverted V, liquid cooled with spar reduction gear. This produces 1,100 bhp. There is provision to fit a cannon firing along the axis of the reduction gear through the airscrew hub. Bosch injection pumps meter the fuel.

The engine is glycol cooled with two radiators, one under each wing close to the trailing edge. Each radiator has a flap, operated by a wheel in the cockpit, which can be used to regulate the cooling. An oil cooler is positioned in a duct beneath the fuselage. The air intake for the supercharger is in the form of a scoop protruding from the left side of the front fuselage. The supercharger is driven through a hydraulic coupling.

Airscrew

The airscrew has three metal blades forming 10.2 ft diameter and is of variable pitch as fitted on most German aircraft of the time. The pitch is controlled electrically.

The pitch can be set between 22.5° and 90° making the airscrew fully feathering. Alterations are performed by a stationery electric motor fixed to the crankcase immediately behind the airscrew hub, this operates through a flexible drive and differential reduction gear. The cockpit has a pitch indicator which is coupled to the electric motor mechanically. The indicator is in the form of clock face with hour and minute hands - one degree being represented by ten 'minutes' on the clock. The pilot has no provision to govern the rpm and must set the pitch accordingly.

Fuselage

The wing-body junction has a very small fillet, the side of the fuselage is roughly normal to the upper surface of the wing. The fuselage's under surface remains flat, flush with the under surface of the wing for more than 3 ft to the rear of the trailing edge. The fuselage cross-section then gradually assumes an ovoid form, finally becoming pear shaped near the tail, the fin is merged gradually into the fuselage.

60 lb of permanent ballast is carried at the back of the fuselage - this is to counteract the extra weight of the DB 601 engine compared to the previously fitted Jumo 210 unit.

The undercarriage attaches to the fuselage at the wing root, retracting sideways into the wings. This allows the aircraft to stand on its undercarriage with the wings removed, this easing maintenance.

Wings
The wings have a straight taper in plan, a sweepback of 1° at the quarter chord line. The wing tips are square cut, the ratio of root chord/tip being 2.06:1.

The thickness chord ratio is 0.148 at the root and 0.105 at the tip. All along the span the aerofoil section has a 2% camber with the maximum thickness at about 30% of the chord. There is no wing twist, the dihedral angle at 5.75° is fairly high.

The surface finish is again good featuring flush riveted metal skin, all inspection doors being flush and well-fitting when closed.

Slots
The slots occupy 46.2% of the span and extend well inboard of the ailerons. The slat is articulated to two transmission rods which run straight out of the wing and are linked together by a robust system of rigid rods and bell-crank levers. The slots open and close very freely and when closed fit very well between the wing and slat. There is no damping device in the mechanism.

Flaps
The 25% slotted flaps occupy 51.8% of the wing span. The ratio of flap area to wing area is 0.14, the maximum angle, 42.5°. The portion of slotted flap immediately behind the radiator is thickened in section to prevent the radiator flap from stalling at when fully open at low climbing speeds. The bulge of the flap considerably reduces the very large expansion at the rear of the radiator duct with the radiator flap open.

Control Surfaces
When tested on the ground the control surfaces showed very little friction and no appreciable backlash. Each surface is mass balanced and the control column is statically balanced for fore and aft movement. This is achieved by using a counterweight incorporated into the elevator control circuit. The transmission system between the cockpit controls and control surfaces in by a mixed system of rods and wires.

Ailerons

The slot width is very small, the ailerons have 21.6% balance and the hinge position is well below the control surface. Each aileron has a mass balance weight of streamlined form carried on an arm projecting downwards. The centre of gravity of the aileron coincides with the hinge line.

When the flaps are up the ailerons have a droop of 1.2° and 2:1 differential - maximum angles are 13.5° down and 25° up. As the flaps are lowered both ailerons come down progressively. When the flaps are fully lowered (42.5°) both ailerons come down to 11°, the differential is now slightly less.

A small fixed trimming tab is attached to each aileron. These tabs are of metal sheet and can be bent on the ground to adjust lateral trim.

Tail Unit

The tailplane is high with a large proportion of the rudder coming below it. It thus remains unshielded at high incidences, useful for anti-spinning. No flight operable rudder trimmer is provided. Controls for the fin and rudder are horn balanced; the percentage balance is 10.35% for the elevator and 8.5% for the rudder. The mass balance weights are carried in the horns.

Longitudinal trimming is effected by means of an adjustable tailplane having a 12° incidence range and is operated mechanically by a handwheel to the pilot's left. This wheel is mounted concentrically with the flap-actuating wheel and by winding both wheels together. The pilot automatically compensates for changes of trim due to the flaps.

Flying the Aircraft

Pilot's View of the Cockpit

Size

The cockpit is certainly too cramped for comfort. The width is too narrow to fit in comfortably or to allow movement within the cockpit. The headroom is also insufficient for taller pilots. When wearing a seat fitted parachute a pilot of average height's head will touch the hood roof. The seat position is also tiring when flying for extended periods.

Noise
The cockpit is noisy at full throttle when compared to a Spitfire.

Main Flying Controls
The control column feels good and the slight offset of the grip eases flying. The rudder pedals are positioned such that the pilot leans back contributing to the lack of comfort during long flights. The pedals cannot be adjusted forwards or backwards to accommodate pilots' varying heights.

Trimming and Flap Controls
These are excellently placed to the pilot's left. The flap gear is manual and extremely good being easy to operate and reliable. A noted feature is the juxtaposition of the tailplane adjusting wheel and the flap control wheel. This means the controls can be operated together with one hand, the change of trim flaps are thereby automatically corrected.

Throttle
The throttle arrangement is extremely simple, consisting of one lever with no gate or override. The DB 601 engine's response to throttle opening is very good due to its direct injection system. This makes it impossible to choke the engine and means it does not splutter or cut out when under negative 'g' if the stick is suddenly pushed forward. This is a crucial factor in air-to-air combat.

Airscrew Control
The works will with no difficulty experienced when in use. The pitch control lever is placed on the dashboard.

Undercarriage Control
This works simply and efficiently, it has no warning hooter as fitted on British aircraft.

Brakes
The brakes are foot operated and work well though do not have very sensitive controls.

Instrument Panel

The instruments are well grouped with the flying instruments to the left and the engine instruments to the right. The dials can be clearly read, illumination for night flying is limited. There is no gyro horizon or blind flying panel.

Ancilliary Equipment

The machine gun and cannon firing switches are positioned in the grip of the stick and are well placed. The electrical panel is to the lower right of the dashboard. The buttons on it are difficult to distinguish for a pilot not experienced on the aircraft. There is a jettison arrangement for the Verey cartridges to allow the pilot to quickly dispose of them in a forced landing. This would prevent the signal of the day being revealed to the enemy.

View

The flat front panel is inclined at 55° to the horizontal when at flying attitude. The larger corner panels are also flat. The left corner panel is divided into two vertical sections. The forward position hinges forward about its leading edge.

For access to the cockpit the hood is hinged on the starboard side. Sliding windows are fitted, one in each of the hood's side panels. For emergency ejection the hood is spring loaded. When the jettison leaver is pushed the whole hood and radio mast are flung clear backwards.

The view when taxiing is poor. This is due to high ground attitude of the aircraft and because the hood cannot be slid backwards to allow the pilot to look out to one side.

When in flight the view is reasonably good. The struts between the glass panel are thin and do not impair vision, catch the pilot's eye or create blind spots.

Lateral and rear vision is fairly good but due to the cramped nature of the cockpit it is difficult to look downward or upwards and behind.

The direct vision opening gives a large field of vision and is completely draft free at all speeds. This allows for high flying speeds to be maintained during heavy rain. The opening also assists landing when the high nose position obstructs forward vision.

The windscreen panels are clear and free from distortion. Oiling up in flight is not a problem. The hood sliding panels are difficult to open particularly at high speeds.

Flight Test

Take-Off
The slotted flaps are set at the recommended position of 20° for take-off. The throttle opens very quickly, responding almost instantaneously to throttle movement. The direct injection system means there is no risk of choking. The initial acceleration is very good and the aircraft will not bucket or swing. When running along the ground the aircraft will rock slightly from side to side but the movement is minimal and should not concern the pilot.

On opening the throttle the stick should be held hard forward. The tail will come up quickly and the stick can then be eased back. The pilot should hold the aircraft on the ground for a short time after flying speed has been reached. If the aeroplane pulls off too soon the left wing will not lift. On applying opposite aileron the wing will come up, fall again with the ailerons snatching somewhat. As long as the aircraft is not pulled off too quickly take-off is fairly easy and straightforward.

The take-off run required is very short and initial rate of climb is fast.

Approach
The stalling speed when gliding, with flaps and undercarriage up, is 75 mph. With flaps and undercarriage down it is 61 mph. Lowering the flaps makes the ailerons heavy and less effective, giving rise to a pronounced nose-down pitching movement. Using the juxtaposing flap and tailplane adjustment operating wheels can easily rectify this. The attitude of the aircraft at constant airspeed changes by roughly 10° when the flaps are put down. Lowering the undercarriage causes slight nose-heaviness.

If the pilot needs to go round again following a failed landing attempt and opens the engine with the flaps down the aircraft will become slightly tail heavy. The aircraft can be held with one hand as the trim is adjusted.

The following table shows the effect of varying the speed of approach as measured when gliding with flaps and undercarriage down. The attitude at cruising level was 5°.

ASI mph	Vi mph	Rate of Descent ft/sec	Gliding Angle	Gliding Attitude
60	80	26.5	13.0°	+3°
70	86	22.5	10.3°	0°
80	93	23.3	9.8°	-5°
90	100	24.5	9.6°	-12°
100	108	29.2	10.5°	-18°

The normal approach speed is 90 mph. At speeds below 80 mph the pilot will gain the impression of sinking, at above 100 mph the impression of diving.

The glide path down is fairly steep at 90 mph; the view is good due to the nose-down attitude. Longitudinal stability is extremely good when flown stick free. The elevator is responsive and heavy at this speed. These features make the ease of approach very good. Ailerons can be lowered to 11° with the flaps without reducing their effectiveness, they will feel much heavier. The rudder is sluggish for small movements.

Normal gliding turns can be performed at 90mph flaps down without any stalling or undue loss of height.

Landing

Landing the Bf 109 is difficult. This is due to two main factors. Firstly the high ground attitude of the aircraft and secondly due to the narrowness of the main undercarriage.

The aircraft must be rotated through a large angle before touchdown requiring a fair amount of skill from the pilot, tempting him to do a wheel landing. If a wheel landing is attempted there is a strong tendency for the left wing to drop just before touchdown. When the ailerons are used quickly to bring the wing up they tend to snatch a little resulting in over-correction. To achieve a three wheel landing the pilot should hold off a little high allowing the aircraft to slowly sink on to the wheels. This eliminates the tendency for the wing to drop. After a few practice landings the pilot should become easily accustomed to the landing technique and have no further problems.

The centre of gravity is unusually far behind the main wheels and the brakes can be fully applied immediately after touchdown, without lifting the tail. The ground run is very short with no tendency to swing or bucket. As the large ground attitude causes the nose of the aircraft to be very high visibility is poor for taxiing. Landing at night is very difficult.

Ground Handling

The Bf 109 can be taxied very fast as the large tail weight prevents it from bouncing or bucketing. Turning rapidly is difficult and a large amount of throttle is required combined with firm use of the differential brakes if attempting to manoeuvre in a tight space. Apart from this turning the ground handling qualities are good. The brakes are powerful and can be used without fear of lifting the tail. The brakes are foot operated.

Trim

Lateral Trim

Each aileron has a small fitted tab that can be easily adjusted when on the ground to correct any imbalance between the wings. The ailerons cannot be trimmed during flight. Speed and throttle settings have no major effect on lateral trim provided the plane is flown without sideslip. The rudder has no trimmer so sideslip quite probable, especially at high speeds when the rudder becomes heavy. Because of the large wing dihedral any inadvertent sideslip produces a pronounced rolling movement. This needs to be corrected by the ailerons.

Directional Trim

There is a large variance in directional trim at different speeds. The absence of a rudder trimmer compounds this problem. When flying at full throttle there is very rapid variation in directional trim with speed. The rudder is light at lower speeds and can be easily held at 5° when climbing at 150 mph. However at high speeds the lack of a rudder trimmer becomes a significant inconvenience to the pilot. At 215 mph the aeroplane is trimmed directionally with no rudder applied. At higher speeds left rudder needs to be applied, at 2° when at 300 mph which requires a large amount of force from the pilot. This can become tiring and reduce the pilot's ability to perform high speed left turns.

Longitudinal Trim

An 11.7" diameter wheel on the pilot's left controls the adjustable tailplane. To move the tailplane through the full angular range, +3.4° to -8.4°, five and three quarter turns are required. Winding the wheel forward pushes the nose down.

The nose down change of trim due to lowering the flaps and undercarriage is large, but readily corrected. The Bf 109 is very stable when gliding at low speeds with flaps down. This reduces manoeuvrability in the looping plane and contributes to the heavy feel of the elevator at high speeds.

'One Control' Tests, Flat Turns and Sideslips

The following tables show the relative degrees of static directional stability and lateral stability. When testing to produce these results the aircraft was trimmed longitudinally to fly straight and level at 230 mph at 10,000 ft at 2,200 rpm. In these conditions slight pressure on the left rudder is required to maintain keep the plane flying straight with no sideslip.

Directional (fixed ailerons) Lateral (fixed rudder)

Sudden application and release of one control with the other fixed

When the rudder is suddenly displaced through half its maximum travel the plane swings through about 8° in yaw and banks 5° in the direction applied to the rudder and the nose pitches downwards slightly.

On releasing the rudder the nose swings back quickly and the plane does an oscillation in yaw and roll, which fades out. During this oscillation the aileron control moves from side to side. With left rudder the left wing slowly comes up and the aircraft enters a right hand spiral.

With right rudder the wing stays down and the plane turns to the right with gradually increasing bank.

When the ailerons are suddenly displaced the plane banks with no opposite yaw.

When the stick is released it immediately returns to the central position. When moved left the left wing rises slowly and the aeroplane banks and turns to the right. When right aileron is applied the right wing stays down and the bank gradually increases. When the ailerons are released the plane is very sensitive to rudder position.

Using the rudder on its own raises the wing.

Steady banked turn with one control, the other being held fixed.
Rudder alone can produce good banked turns when the ailerons are fixed centrally. Quarter rudder is required to initiate the turn and very little sideslip results. To recover from the turn half rudder should be applied. If the rudder is applied harshly more sideslip is produced on entry and recovery. This also produces a pronounced nose- down pitching moment which has to be corrected by pulling the stick back.

If the rudder is released during a 30° banked turn to left the plane rolls slowly to the right. When rudder is released in a 30° banked right turn the result is an increase in bank and tightening of the turn.

Ailerons alone can produce excellent banked turns. Very little sideslip is produced when entering or leaving the turn, even if the ailerons are used harshly.

Flat Turns and Sideslips

Undercarriage Up:

Flown at 230 mph at 10,000 ft
Only half rudder was used for the test. Full rudder can be applied using considerable force. This produces considerable nose-down pitching movement so that excessive pull has to be applied to the stick to hold the nose up.

Steady Sideslip when Gliding, Flaps & Undercarriage Up

Gliding at 100 mph:
The maximum bank angle in a straight sideslip is 5°. Rudder is the limiting control, quarter aileron should be used to hold the wing

down against full rudder. The aeroplane is nose heavy during side-slip. It also vibrates and will feel a little unsteady, requiring occasional reaction from the controls to keep speed constant.

If all controls are released during side-slip the nose falls and the plane will swing smartly into the sideslip path and bank will decrease very quickly. The plane will then glide straight with level wings and the nose will slowly rise to the trimmed position and oscillate fractionally in pitch.

Steady Sideslip when Gliding, Flaps & Undercarriage Down

Gliding at 90 mph:
The maximum bank angle is again 5°, with rudder the limiting control. One fifth aileron is required in conjunction with full opposite rudder. The aircraft is less nose-heavy with flaps up. Vibration again occurs and the plane will feel unsteady.

When all controls are released the same effect occurs as above but with increased pitching oscillation which also lasts longer.

Stalling Tests

Stalling Speeds and CL Max

Condition		Pilot's A.S.I. mph	
Indicated Airspeed mph		CL	
Flaps & Ailerons	Undercarriage	Speed at which slots open	Stalling Speed
Speed at which slots open	Stalling Speed	CL at which slots open	CL Max.
Up	Up	111	754
120.5	95.5	0.865	1.4
Down: Flaps 42.5° Ailerons 10°	Up	90	61
100.5	81	1.2	1.9
Down: Flaps 42.5° Ailerons 10°	Down	90	61
100.5	81	1.2	1.9

High Speed Dives

The plane was put into a 370 mph dive, then all three controls were in turn displaced slightly and then released. No vibration, flutter of snaking develops.

With elevator trimmed for normal level flight at full throttle a fairly large push is needed to hold the plane in a dive. If the trimmer is wound forward recovery from the dive is very difficult due to the excessive heaviness of the elevator at high speeds.

When 370 mph is reached considerable pressure is needed on the left rudder bar to keep the plane straight. If the rudder is released the plane will bank and turn to the right. Small rudder movements, sufficient for 10° yaw will not produce a pitching movement. Large rudder displacements will cause the nose to pitch down.

Flying Controls

Ailerons
Aileron control is very good at low speeds, there is positive feel and a definite resistance to stick movement.

As speed rises the ailerons gradually become heavier but retain excellent response, being at their best between 150 and 200 mph. Between 200 and 300 mph they become noticeably heavier and over 300 mph become too heavy for comfortable manoeuvring. Over 400 mph the pilot can exert up to one fifth aileron using all his strength.

Throttling back will not alter the effectiveness of ailerons at any speed. At low speeds lowering the flaps (ailerons come down 11° with the flaps) results in the ailerons becoming much heavier and slightly reduces their effectiveness.

The ailerons can snatch as the wing tip slots open. This is pronounced during manoeuvring. For instance is the stick is pulled back during a tight turn, producing additional 'g', the slots will open at high airspeeds. As they open the stick will snatch laterally through several inches in either direction. This snatch is sufficient to spoil a pilot's aim during a dogfight.

Some snatching will also occur when gliding close to stall speeds with flaps up and slots open. This will disappear when the flaps are fully lowered, so shouldn't concern the pilot during the approach glide.

Elevator
The elevator gives exceptionally good control as low speeds. It is fairly heavy and not too sensitive during the approach glide with excellent response. Over 250 mph the aileron becomes much heavier and between 300 and 400 mph restricts manoeuvrability during looping.

At low speeds the elevator is slightly lighter if the engine is throttled back and slightly less responsive. Lowering the flaps will not effect the elevator control.

Rudder
The rudder is light but sluggish at slow speeds, large displacements will be needed to produce quick response. As speed increases so will rudder response. Between 200 and 300 mph the rudder is the lightest of all the controls for small movements so should be used for directional aim during dog-fights. Over 300 mph the lack of a directional trimmer will be felt as a small amount of left rudder needs to be applied to prevent side-slip. Constantly applying this rudder can cause the pilot to become tired.

Throttling back at slow speeds will make the rudder a little more sluggish. Lowering the flaps further reduces rudder effectiveness though response is still adequate with larger displacements.

If speed is increased while gliding with flaps down the rudder will start juddering slightly at 100 mph. The juddering increases rapidly as speed rises and makes increasing speed to over 120 mph inadvisable. The normal approach speed with flaps down should be 90 mph, rudder vibration is not noticed at this speed.

Harmony
Between 150 and 250 mph the controls are well harmonised, the elevator being the heaviest. At low speeds the sluggishness of the rudder adversely affects harmony. At very high speeds the heaviness of the ailerons mars harmony.

General Flying Impression
Test pilots particularly liked the positive feel of the Bf 109's controls at low and medium speeds. Features they disliked were the undue stiffening of the controls at high speeds, particularly the ailerons. Also the aileron snatching caused by slots opening while diving. The lack of a rudder trimmer was also considered a major shortcoming.

Aerobatics
Loops must be started from around 280 mph. Slots can open near the top of the loop resulting in aileron snatching and loss of direction. This impedes accurate looping.

Rolls can be performed very easily at speeds below 250 mph when the ailerons are light and very effective. There is a tendency for the nose to fall at the final stages of a roll, meaning the stick must be pulled well back in order to keep the nose up. Upward rolls are more difficult. At high speeds the heaviness of the elevator means only a gentle pull-out from a dive is possible.

Messerschmitt Bf 109 *v.* Spitfire I

Comparative Aileron Characteristics

	Bf109E	Spitfire Mk I
Maximum Sideways Force average pilot can apply to stick	40	60
Time to 45° bank when applied at 400 mph	4	4
Corresponding Aileron Displacement	1/5	1/5
Kb2 at 400 mph	-0.145	-0.14
Wing Span ft	32.4	37.0
Aileron Type	Slotted	Frise
% Balance (area ahead hinge/ total area)	21.6	27.5
Total aileron area/gross wing area	0.0655	0.078
Max. stick travel in.	+/- 4	+/- 8
Max. aileron angles Up	25°	25°
Down	13.5°	19°

Turns at Minimum Radius without Height Loss
Both aeroplanes were tested at full throttle at 12,000 ft altitude.

	Bf109E	Spitfire Mk I
Minimum Radius of turn without loss of height, feet	885	696
Corresponding time to turn through 360°, seconds	25	19
Indicated Airspeed Vi, mph	129	133
Pilot's ASI, mph	118	126
'G'	2.10	2.65
Angle of Bank	62°	68°

Tester's Comments
The strengths and weaknesses of the Bf 109E were summarised as follows:

Strengths:
- (i)   High top speed and excellent rate of climb
- (ii)   Good control at low speeds
- (iii) Gentle stall, even under 'g'
- (iv) Engine does not cut immediately under negative 'g'

Weaknesses:
- (i)   Controls, particularly the ailerons, are heavy at high speeds
- (ii)   High wing loading causes the aeroplane to stall under 'g' and gives it relatively wide turning circle
- (iii) Aileron snatching occurs as the slots open
- (iv) Fast manoeuvres at high speed are difficult
- (v)   Absence of a rudder trimmer curtails stability to bank left at high speeds
- (vi) Cockpit too cramped for comfort during combat

The gentle stall and good control under 'g' enable the pilot to get the most from the aircraft during dog-fighting by flying very near to the stall. This allows the Bf 109 to remain on the tail of a Spitfire. Both the Bf 109 and Spitfire suffer from the inability to roll fast at high speeds because of the heavy ailerons.

Handling Summary
- (i)   Take-off is fairly easy and straightforward. The controls have excellent feel and the plane is very stable in a glide. Landing can be difficult for pilots unused to the aircraft. Taxiing characteristics are good.
- (ii)   Absence of a rudder trimmer is a handicap at high speeds as there is a large variance in directional trim as speed changes. Longitudinally the aircraft is very stable.
- (iii) Good banked turns can be achieved using ailerons or rudder alone. Sideslip produces a large nose-down pitching moment.
- (iv) The stall is not violent and there is no tendency to spin. CL maximum when gliding is 1.4 with flaps up. 1.9 with flaps down.
- (v)   There is no vibrating or snaking when controls are displaced slightly during a high-speed dive.

(vi)   Aileron snatching occurs when the slots are open. All three controls are heavy at high speeds.

Messerschmitt Me 109 G-2 Technical Description and Notes

Dimensions and Areas

Main Airframe Dimensions and Areas

Wing Span	32.6 ft
Length	29.3 ft
Undercarriage Track	6.5 ft
Mean Wing Chord	5.7 ft
Wing Area	172 sq ft
Total Flap Area	11.2 sq. ft
Total Slot Area	6.7 ft
Total Radiator Flap Area	8.6 ft
Total Area of Ailerons	8.3 sq. ft
Span of Tail Unit	9.8 ft
Tailplane Area	15.7 sq. ft
Elevator Area	9.25 sq. ft
Fin Area	7.5 sq. ft
Rudder Area	5.9 sq. ft

Undercarriage

Undercarriage Leg	VDM 8-2787-05
Tyre Size	650 x 150 (Conti, Metzeler, Dunlop)
Tyre Pressure	64 lb/sq. in.

Pressure in oleo-leg (no load): 355 lb/sq. in.

Tail Wheel
Leg with helical spring and hydraulic damping
Tyre Size: 290 x 110
Tyre Pressure   64 lb/sq. in.

Propeller
Three-blade propeller, type VDM 9-12087 A.
Clockwise rotation as viewed from pilot's cockpit
Weight including blades, hub and vp mechanism: 375 lb
Diameter   9.8 ft

Engine
Daimler-Benz DB 605, B series. Inverted V 12-cylinder, liquid cooled.
Volumetric Compression Ratio: 7.3–7.5
Reduction Gear Ratios: 1–1.875
The maximum permissible engine speed in level flight is 2,800 rpm and 3,000 rpm during a dive.
Octane Fuel Rating used: 87

Engine Ratings

Rating	RPM	Boost		Altitude	Power	Fuel Consumption
		ata	lb/sq. in.	Ft	bhp	Gallon/hour
Take-Off	2,800	1.42	+5.5	SL	1,455	102.5
Climb (30 mins)	2,600	1.30	+3.8	SL	1,290	85.5
Max. Continuous	2,300	1.15	+1.7	SL	1,060	68.75
Max. Emergency	2,800	1.42	+5.5	18,700	1,335	93.75
Combat (30 min)	2,600	1.30	+3.8	19,000	1,235	81.5
Max. Continuous	2,300	1.15	+1.7	18,000	1,065	69.25
Economical	2,100	1.00	-0.5	18,700	880	54.25

Oil Cooler
Type - SKF/Behr FO 820
The cooling surface is 125 sq. ft, capacity 0.9 gallon and the weight 60 lb. The test pressure is given as 71 lb/sq. in.

Coolant Radiators
Two light metal radiators, type SKF/Behr A1.F.750B.
The coolant is a mixture of water and glycol.

Cooling surface area: 125 sq. ft
Capacity: 1.1 gal
Test Pressure: 28.4 lb/sq. in.

Header Tanks
Two light metal header tanks fitted, type NKF.
Capacity: 1.1 gal coolant, 1.1 gal air space
Total Weight: 7.3 lb
Test Pressure: 17 lb/sq. in.

Oil Tanks
One light metal oil tanks, type NKF.
Oil Capacity: 8.1 gal plus additional air space of 1.3 gal
Weight: 12.75 lb
Test Pressure: 5 lb/sq. in.

Fuel Tanks
One fuel tank manufacture by Karl Otto Raspe & Co.
Capacity: 88 gallons
Weight: 121 lb
Test Pressure: 2.8 lb/sq. in

Jettisonable Fuel Tank
One jettisonable fuel tank fitted, type Ju 87/NKF.
Capacity: 65 gallons
Weight: 55 lb
Test Pressure: 2.8 lb/sq. in.

Weights

Weights (lb)		Fighter			Fighter-Bomber	
	3 Guns no Drop Tank	2 additional wing guns	3 Guns and Drop Tank	With 1 x 250 kg bomb	With 5 x 50 kg bombs	
Empty	4,938	4,938	4,938	4,938	4,938
Flying 6,678	7,151	7,238	7,291	7,205	
Maximum Flying Weight:	7,606				

Speeds

Engine Boost ata	Rating RPM	Altitude ft	Max Speed mph
1.30	2,700	SL	305

1.30	2,700	23,500	375
1.30	2,700	30,000	364
1.42	2,800	SL	317
1.42	2,800	23,000	384
1.42	2,800	30,000	372

Climb

Engine Boost ata	Rating RPM	Altitude ft	Rate of Climb ft/min
1.30	2,750	SL	3,350
1.30	2,750	21,500	3,400
1.30	2,750	30,000	1,400
1.42	2,800	SL	3,950
1.42	2,800	21,000	3,800

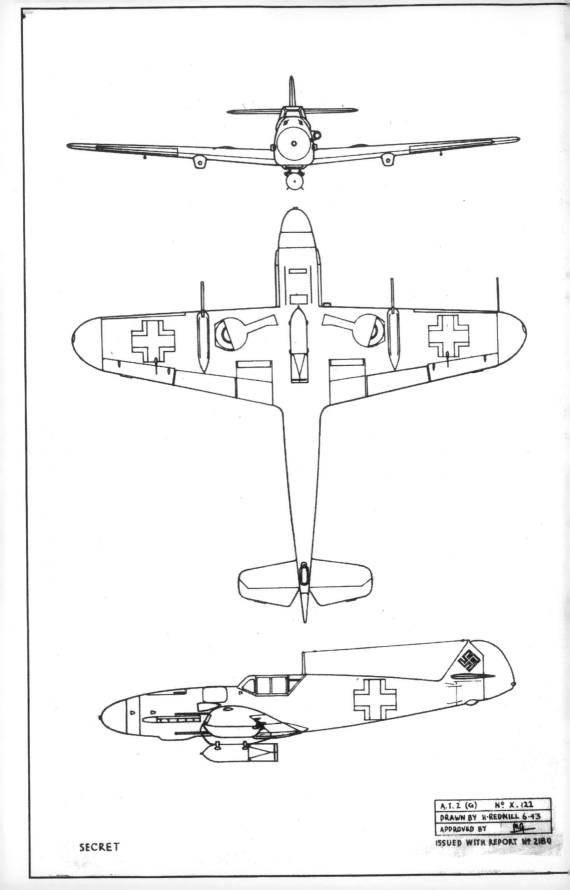

SECRET

A.T.2 (G)	Nº X.122
DRAWN BY H·REDMILL 6·43	
APPROVED BY	MG

ISSUED WITH REPORT Nº 2180

FIG. 3

ME 109   COCKPIT

Hurricane

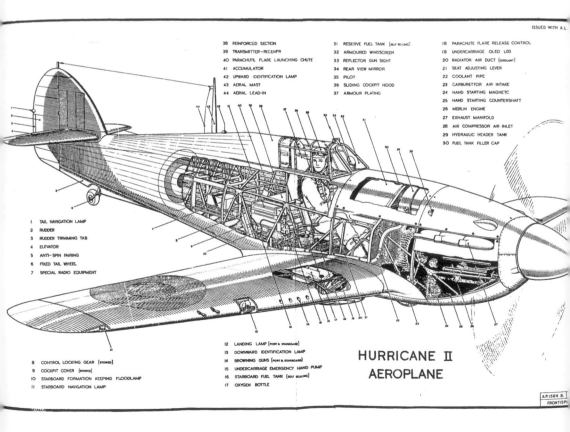

38 REINFORCED SECTION
39 TRANSMITTER—RECEIVER
40 PARACHUTE. FLARE LAUNCHING CHUTE
41 ACCUMULATOR
42 UPWARD IDENTIFICATION LAMP
43 AERIAL MAST
44 AERIAL LEAD-IN

31 RESERVE FUEL TANK [SELF SEALING]
32 ARMOURED WINDSCREEN
33 REFLECTOR GUN SIGHT
34 REAR VIEW MIRROR
35 PILOT
36 SLIDING COCKPIT HOOD
37 ARMOUR PLATING

18 PARACHUTE FLARE RELEASE CONTROL
19 UNDERCARRIAGE OLEO LEG
20 RADIATOR AIR DUCT [COOLANT]
21 SEAT ADJUSTING LEVER
22 COOLANT PIPE
23 CARBURETTOR AIR INTAKE
24 HAND STARTING MAGNETO
25 HAND STARTING COUNTERSHAFT
26 MERLIN ENGINE
27 EXHAUST MANIFOLD
28 AIR COMPRESSOR AIR INLET
29 HYDRAULIC HEADER TANK
30 FUEL TANK FILLER CAP

1 TAIL NAVIGATION LAMP
2 RUDDER
3 RUDDER TRIMMING TAB
4 ELEVATOR
5 ANTI–SPIN FAIRING
6 FIXED TAIL WHEEL
7 SPECIAL RADIO EQUIPMENT

8 CONTROL LOCKING GEAR [STOWED]
9 COCKPIT COVER [STOWED]
10 STARBOARD FORMATION KEEPING FLOODLAMP
11 STARBOARD NAVIGATION LAMP

12 LANDING LAMP [PORT & STARBOARD]
13 DOWNWARD IDENTIFICATION LAMP
14 BROWNING GUNS [PORT & STARBOARD]
15 UNDERCARRIAGE EMERGENCY HAND PUMP
16 STARBOARD FUEL TANK [SELF SEALING]
17 OXYGEN BOTTLE

HURRICANE II
AEROPLANE

NOTES TO OFFICIAL USERS

Air Ministry Orders and Vol. II leaflets as issued from time to time may affect the subject matter of this publication. It should be understood that amendment lists are not always issued to bring the publication into line with the orders or leaflets and it is for holders of this book to arrange the necessary link-up.

Where an order or leaflet contradicts any portion of this publication, an amendment list will generally be issued, but when this is not done, the order or leaflet must be taken as the **over**riding authority.

Where amendment action has taken place, the number of the amendment list concerned will be found at the top of each page affected, and amendments of technical importance will be indicated by a vertical line on the left-hand side of the text against the matter amended or added. Vertical lines relating to previous amendments to a page are not repeated. If complete revision of any division of the book (e.g. a Chapter) is made this will be indicated in the title page for that division and the vertical lines will not be employed.

December 1940

AIR PUBLICATION 1564B
Pilot's Notes

LIST OF SECTIONS

(A detailed Contents List appears at
the beginning of each Section)

R.T.P./722. 4500. 12/40.

Hurricane

Revised in Vol. I by A.L.42
and in Pilot's Notes by A.L/P.

AIR PUBLICATION 1564B & D
Volume I and Pilot's Notes.

SECTION I

PILOT'S CONTROLS AND EQUIPMENT

LIST OF CONTENTS

Revised in Vol. I by A.L.42   A.P. 1564B & D SECT. 1.
and in Pilot's Notes by A.L/P.   Volume I and Pilot's Notes.

INTRODUCTION

1. The Hurricane Mks. II and IV are each fitted with a Merlin
    20 engine and a Rotol 35° propeller. The Mks. IID and IV
    are low-level attack versions of the earlier Marks and are
    equipped to carry various alternative armaments. The
    aircraft controls including the undercarriage, flaps and
    brakes are identical with those on Mark I aircraft.

FUEL, OIL AND COOLANT SYSTEMS

2. Fuel tanks (See Fig. 5 and 5A)

    (i)   Main and Reserve tanks - The main tanks are housed
          within the centre section, one on each side of the
          fuselage, and a reserve tank is carried between the
          fireproof bulkhead and the instrument panel. Fuel
          is delivered to the engine by an engine-driven pump.
          These tanks are self-sealing and their effective
          capacities are as follows:

                    Main tanks: 33 gallons each
                    Reserve tank: 28 gallons

          To meet the possibility of engine cutting due to
          fuel boiling in warm weather at high altitudes, these
          tanks can be pressurised (operative above 20,000 feet).
          Pressurising, however, impairs the self-sealing of
          tanks and should, therefore, be used only when the
          fuel pressure warning light comes on, or when auxiliary
          drop tanks are used (see below).

    (ii) Auxiliary tanks: When not fitted with underwing armament
          or containers, a pair of auxiliary tanks may be carried
          one under each wing. The types of tank and their
          capacities are as follows:

                    Fixed: 44 gallons each
                    Drop: 45 or 90 gallons each

          With the exception of some fixed tanks which are used
          for combat duties, these tanks are non-self-sealing.
          Fuel in the fixed tanks is delivered to the main tanks
          by electrically driven emmersed pumps, but fuel in the
          drop tanks is supplied direct to the engine fuel pump
          by air pressure.

F.S/2.

3. Fuel cocks:

    (i) The main fuel cock control (48) on the left-hand
         side of the cockpit has a spring safety plate which
         prevents the fuel supply being turned off inadvertently.
         The control can only be turned to the OFF position
         whilst the safety plate is held depressed.

    (ii) A switch for the electric pump in each fixed auxiliary
          tank is fitted on the left-hand side of the cockpit,
          either just above the elevator trimming tab control,
          or on the lower part of the electrical panel.

    (iii) The fuel cock control (73) and jettison lever (74)
           for the drop tanks are mounted together on the right-
           hand side of the cockpit, below the windscreen
           de-icing pump. The cock control has three positions:
           OFF, PORT and STARBOARD. The pressurising cock must
           be turned on when the tanks are used. The jettison
           lever is pulled down to jettison both tanks simultan-
           eously, but cannot be moved until the fuel cock is
           set to OFF. When the lever is operated, the air
           pressure supply is automatically cut off.

    (iv) The tank pressurising cock (22) is fitted on the
          left-hand-side of the cockpit, below the throttle
          quadrant, and is marked ATMOSPHERE and PRESSURE.

4. Fuel contents gauge: A gauge (49) on the right-hand side
    of the instrument panel indicates selectively the contents
    of each of the three main tanks. A switch unit (48),
    comprising a combined selector and pushbutton, is fitted
    above the gauge.

5. Fuel pressure warning light: The warning light (50) on the
    right-hand side of the instrument panel comes on if the
    pressure drops to 6lb./sq.in.

6. Oil system: The self-sealing oil tank, which has an effective
    capacity of 9 gallons, forms the port leading edge of the
    centre section. The oil passes through a filter before
    entering the engine and then through a cooler insider the
    coolant radiator. Pressure (54) and temperature (53) gauges
    are fitted on the instrument panel. When 90 gallon fuel
    drop tanks are carried, an auxiliary oil tank of 4 gallons
    capacity is fitted behind the seat, the cock control for
    which is on the left-hand side of the seat, above the
    radiator flap control quadrant.

Revised in Vol. I by A.L.42   A.P. 1564B & D Sect. 1.
and in Pilot's Notes by A.L/P.   Volume I and Pilot's Notes.

7. Coolant system: The system is thermostatically controlled,
    the radiator being by-passed until the coolant reaches a
    certain temperature. The header tank is mounted on the
    fireproof bulkhead and is fitted with a pressure relief
    valve. The air flow through the radiator is controlled
    by a flap lever in the cockpit.

MAIN SERVICES

8. Hydraulic system: An engine-driven hydraulic pump supplies
    the power for operating the under-carriage and flaps. The
    system is automatic, selection of the desired operation of
    the undercarriage or flaps, by means of the selector lever,
    being sufficient to commence the operation. A handpump (71)
    is provided for use in the event of engine failure or engine
    driven pump failure.

9. Electrical system: A 12-volt generator, controlled by a
    switch (3) on the left-hand side of the cockpit, supplies
    an accumulator which in turn supplies the whole of the
    electrical installation. There is a voltmeter (31) on
    the left-hand side of the cockpit, and a red light (36)
    marked POWER FAILURE on the instrument panel comes on when
    the generator is not charging the accumulator.

10. Pneumatic system: The wheel brakes and the gun-firing
    mechanism are operated pneumatically, air being supplied by
    an engine-driven compressor and stored in a cylinder at a
    maximum pressure of 300 lb./sq.in.

AIRCRAFT CONTROLS

11. Flying controls: The control column is of the spade-grip
    pattern and incorporates a gun-firing pushbutton and the
    brake lever. The rudder bar is adjustable for leg reach by
    means of a starwheel midway between the two pedals.

12. Trimming tabs: The elevator trimming tabs are controlled
    by a handwheel (24) on the left-hand side of the cockpit and
    an indicator is fitted next to it. Forward rotation of the
    hand-wheel corrects tail heaviness. The automatic balance
    tab on the rudder can be set for trimming purposes by means
    of a small control wheel (23) on the left-hand side of the
    cockpit which is turned clockwise to apply right rudder.

13. Undercarriage and flap control: The selector lever (76)
    for the undercarriage and flaps is on the right-hand side
    of the cockpit and works in a gate, having a neutral position
    for both undercarriage and flaps, the positions for operating
    the flaps being outboard. The catch on the side of the lever
    must be pressed in order to release it for movement from an

F.S./3

operative position, but the lever can be moved from the
neutral position without first releasing the catch. To
obviate inadvertent selection on the ground of the wheels
up position, a safety catch (77) is provided on the gate
which must be turned in a clockwise direction to permit
entry of the selector lever into the wheels UP slot. For
emergency lowering of the undercarriage see Para. 35.

14. Undercarriage indicator: The electrical indicator (41)
is on the left-hand side of the instrument panel and has
duplicate pairs of lamps, the green lamps indicating when
the undercarriage is locked in the DOWN position and the
red lamps when the undercarriage is fully retracted and
locked. There are two switches to the left of the indicator,
the left-hand one (38) being the ON-OFF switch for the green
lamps, and the right-hand one (39) being the change-over
switch for the duplicate sets of lamps. A dimmer switch
is provided in the centre of the indicator. When the undercarriage is retracted, the wheels are visible through two
small windows in the bottom of the cockpit.

15. Undercarriage warning light: A red light on the instrument
panel comes on at any time when the throttle lever is less
than one third open and the undercarriage is not locked
down. When the throttle is opened again or the undercarriage
is lowered the light goes out.

16. Flap indicator: This (72) is mechanically operated, the
pointer moving along a graduated scale marked UP and DOWN
at its extremities. It is situated immediately below the
hydraulic selector lever.

17. Wheel brakes: The brake lever is fitted on the control column
spade-grip and a catch for retaining it in the on position
for parking is fitted below the lever pivot. A triple
pressure gauge, showing the air-pressure in the pneumatic
system cylinder and at each brake, is mounted forward of the
foot of the control column.

18. Flying control locking gear: The locking struts, interference
bar and bracket are stowed in a canvas bag in the starboard
side of the wireless bay. The bracket clips on to the control

Revised in Vol. I by A.L.42
and in Pilot's Notes by A.L/P

A.P. 1564B & D Sect. 1.
Volume I and Pilot's Notes.

column, just below the spade grip, for locking of the
aileron control and the two struts, attached to the
bracket by shackles, lock the rudder bar and control
column. The spring loaded interference bar fits on to
the bracket and is inserted in a slot in the back of the
seat.

ENGINE CONTROLS

19. Throttle: The throttle lever (7) works in a slot in
the decking shelf on the left-hand side of the cockpit.
The take-off position is gated. There is a friction
adjuster (16) on the inboard end of the lever spindle.
The mixture control is fully automatic and there is no
pilot's control lever.

20. Boost control cut-out: The automatic boost control may
be cut out by pulling the knob (34) on the left-hand
side of the instrument panel.

21. Propeller control: The speed control lever (10) on the
left-hand side of the cockpit varies the governed rpm
from 3,000 down to 1,800. A friction adjuster is fitted
on the inboard side of the control.

22. Supercharger control: The push-pull control (17) is fitted
below the left-hand side of the instrument panel, and must
be pushed in for low (M) gear and pulled out for high (S)
gear

23. Radiator flap control: The airflow through the coolant
radiator and oil cooler is controlled by a lever (26) on
the left-hand side of the pilot's seat. In order to
release the lever for operation the thumb-button must be
depressed.

24. Slow-running cut-out: The control on the carburettor is
operated by pulling out the knob (64) immediately to the
right of the undercarriage and flap selector lever.

25. Cylinder priming pump: The priming pump (59) is fitted
below the right-hand side of the instrument panel.

26. <u>Engine starting</u>:   The starter and booster coil push-
    buttons (32 & 33) are to the left of the ignition
    switches (58) on the instrument panel.   An external
    supply socket for the starter motor is accessible
    through a removable panel in the starboard engine
    cowling, and two handles for hand starting are stowed
    in the undercarriage wheel recess under the centre
    section.

27. <u>Oil dilution</u>:   The pushbutton (4) for operating the
    solenoid valve is on the left-hand side of the cockpit.

    OTHER CONTROLS

28. <u>Gun controls</u>:   The machine guns and cannon are normally
    fired by the pushbutton on the control column spade grip.
    The two 40 m.m. guns on MK IID and IV aircraft are fired
    electro-pneumatically by the pushbutton in the throttle
    lever; they cannot be fired, however, until the master
    switch (11) on the decking shelf, forward of the throttle
    quadrant, is switched on.   The cocking lever (28) on the
    electrical panel to the left of the seat should be pushed
    down in the event of a misfire.

29. <u>R.P. controls</u>:   The projectiles are fired by the pushbutton
    in the throttle lever and a selector switch (40) below the
    left-hand side of the windscreen enables them to be fired
    in PAIRS or as a SALVO.   They must not be fired with the
    flaps lowered.

30. <u>Bomb controls</u>:   There are two selector switches and two
    nose and tail fusing switches on a small panel (67) on the
    right-hand side of the cockpit.   The bombs are released by
    the pushbutton in the throttle lever.

31. <u>S.C.I. controls</u>:   These are operated by the pushbutton in
    the throttle lever and there is a container jettison push-
    button (63) on the right-hand side of the cockpit.

32. <u>Camera gun control</u>:   The camera gun operates only when the
    guns and cannon or the R.P. are fired, or when the lower
    pushbutton on the control column spade grip is depressed.

Revised in Vol. I by A.L.42.   A.P.1564B & D Sect. 1.
and in Pilot's Notes by A.L/P.   Volume I and Pilot's Notes.

33. Landing lamps: The landing lamps, one in the leading edge
     of each wing, are controlled by a two-way switch (15) to
     the left of the instrument panel, which enables either
     lamp to be used; both lamps are off when the switch is in
     the upright position. A dipping lever (5) on the left-hand
     side of the cockpit can be held in any position by tightening
     the knurled wheel; when the wheel is unscrewed, the lever
     is pulled aft into the UP position by a return spring in each
     of the lamp units.

34. Recognition device: The flares are selected and released
     by a single lever (25) immediately aft of the trimming tab
     control   The slot is marked SELECT and FIRE.

     EMERGENCIES

35. Undercarriage emergency operation:

     (i)   In the event of failure of the engine-driven hydraulic
            pump, the undercarriage may be lowered by moving the
            selector lever to the WHEELS DOWN position and then
            operating the handpump.

     (ii)   If the handpump fails to lower the undercarriage the
            selector lever should still be left in the WHEELS DOWN
            position and the red-painted foot pedal (21), outboard
            of the port heelrest, should be firmly pushed forward.
            The wheels should then fall and lock down under their
            own weight.

     (iii) If difficulty is experienced in operating the under-
            carriage and flap selector lever it may be overcome by
            first selecting the opposite to that which is required.
            If, for example, the selection of undercarriage down
            is found to be difficult, the lever should first be
            moved into the undercarriage up position and then
            immediately moved to the down position.

36. Hood jettisoning: To jettison the hood the lever aft of
     the radiator flap control should be pulled sharply forward
     and upwards. If the hood does not readily leave the air-
     craft it should be assisted by pushing it upwards, or
     failing that, by releasing the emergency exit panel (see
     below) in addition to operating the jettison control.

     Note: When jettisoning the hood it is advisable to lower
            one's head as far as possible so as to avoid injury
            when it leaves the aircraft.

F.S/5

37. <u>Emergency exit panel</u>: The large detachable panel on the starboard side of the cockpit is secured by horizontal spring-loaded plungers and a bolt operated by the cockpit hood. To jettison the panel, the hood must first be fully opened and the release lever (66) then moved aft and upwards.

38. <u>Abandoning by parachute</u>: When abandoning the aircraft by parachute it is important to decrease speed and then dive over the side immediately. The pilot must not stand on the seat and delay in jumping or he will hit either the aerial mast or the tailplane.

39. <u>Forced landing</u>: In the event of having to make a forced landing the glide may be lengthened considerably by moving the propeller speed control fully back and gliding at about 130 mph IAS. With undercarriage and flaps up the gliding angle at speeds of 120-140 mph IAS is very flat.

40. <u>Ditching</u> (See A.P.2095 Pilot's Notes General)

    (i)   In general the pilot should, if possible, abandon the aircraft by parachute.

    (ii)   In the event of having to ditch, auxiliary drop tanks, bombs or containers (if fitted) should be jettisoned and the following procedure should be observed:

           (a)   The cockpit hood should be jettisoned

           (b)   Flaps should be lowered fully in order to reduce landing speed as much as possible

           (c)   The undercarriage should be retracted

           (d)   Safety harness should be kept on, with straps tight, and the R/T plug disconnected

           (e)   The engine, if available, should be used to help make the touch-down in a tail-down attitude at as low a speed as possible

           (f)   When about to touch the water a normal banked turn, with full rudder, should be made so as to prevent 'hooking' the radiator into the water

110

Revised in Vol. I by A.L.42
and in Pilot's Notes by A.L/P

A.P. 1564B & D Sect. 1.
Volume I and Pilot's Notes.

41. <u>First-aid outfit</u>: The first-aid outfit is attached to the inside of a detachable panel on the port side of the cockpit and is accessible by kicking in the panel breaking the stringers, and tearing the fabric.

42. <u>Crowbar</u>: A crowbar, for use in an emergency, is stowed in clips to the right of the seat.

KEY TO FIG. 1

1. Radio contactor master switch
2. Cockpit light dimmer switch
3. Generator switch
4. Oil dilution pushbutton
5. Landing lamp control lever
6. Oxygen supply cock
7. Throttle lever (incorporating pushbutton)
8. Socket for footage indicator plug
9. Wedge plate for camera gun footage indicator
10. Propeller speed control
11. Cannon master switch
12. Compass light dimmer switch
13. Cockpit light dimmer switch
14. Landing lamp switch
15. Friction adjuster
16. Supercharger control
17. Fuel cock control
18. R.T. VO contactor switch
19. Radio contactor
20. R.T. push-button
21. Undercarriage emergency release lever
22. Fuel tank pressurising control
23. Rudder trimming tab control
24. Elevator trimming tab control
25. Recognition device selector lever
26. Heated clothing socket
27. Radiator flap control lever
28. Cannon control lever
29. Microphone/telephone socket
30. Hood catch control
31. Voltmeter

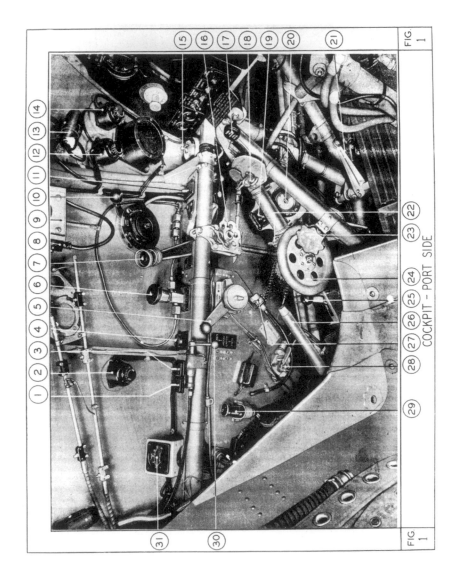

COCKPIT – PORT SIDE

FIG. 1

112

KEY TO FIG. 2

A.P. 1564B & D Sect 1,
Volume 2 and Pilot's Notes
and in Vol. 1 by A.L.42
in Pilot's Notes by A.L.2F

32. Engine starter pushbutton
33. Booster coil pushbutton
34. Beam approach control
35. Open regulator
36. Power failure warning light
37. Cockpit ventilator
38. Undercarriage indicator ON-OFF switch
39. Undercarriage indicator change-over switch
40. R.P. selector switch
41. Undercarriage position indicator
42. Instrument flying panel
43. Reflector sight spare bulbs gauge
44. Engine speed indicator
45. Reflector sight switch
46. Cockpit ventilator
47. Boost gauge
48. Fuel contents gauge selector switch
49. Fuel contents gauge
50. Fuel pressure warning light
51. Radiator temperature gauge
52. Beam approach master switch
53. Oil temperature gauge
54. Oil pressure gauge
55. Carburettor mixture
56. Navigation lights switch
57. Pressure head heater switch
58. Ignition switches

INSTRUMENT PANEL

FIG. 2

FIG. 2

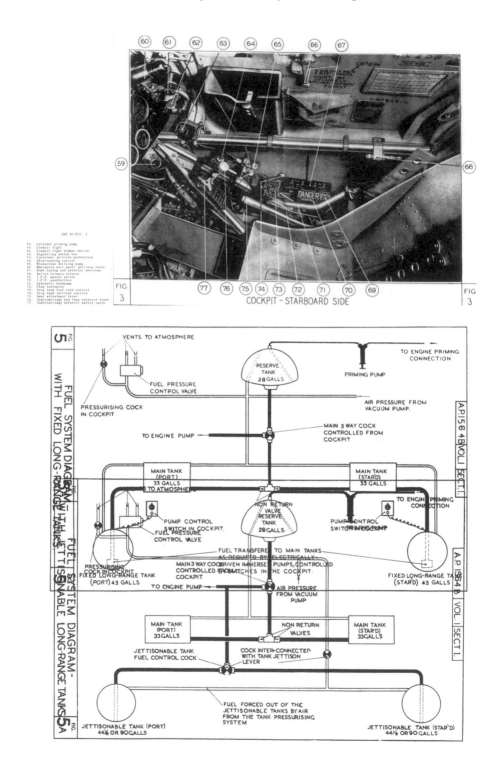

KEY TO FIG. 3

59. Cylinder priming pump
60. Cockpit light
61. Cockpit light dimmer switch
62. Signalling switch box
63. Container jettison pushbutton
64. Slow-running cut-out
65. Windscreen de-icing pump
66. Emergency exit panel jettison lever
67. Bomb fusing and selector switches
68. Sutton harness release
69. I.F.F. master switch
70. I.F.F. pushbuttons
71. Hydraulic handpump
72. Flap indicator
73. Drop tank fuel cock control
74. Drop tank jettison control
75. Seat adjustment lever
76. Undercarriage and flap selector lever
77. Undercarriage selector safety catch

FIG. 3

COCKPIT – STARBOARD SIDE

FIG 3

Hurricane

AIR PUBLICATION 1564B + D
VOLUME I AND PILOTS NOTES

SECTION 2
Handling and Flying Notes

1. Engine Data

2. Flying Limitations

3. Position Error Corrections

4. Management of Fuel and Oil Systems

5. Preliminaries

6. Starting the Engine and Warming Up

7. Testing the Engine and Installations

8. Check List before Take-Off

9. Take-Off

10. Climbing

11. General Flying

12. Maximum Performance

13. Economical Flying

14. Stalling

15. Spinning

16. Aerobatics

17. Diving

18. Check List before Landing

19. Approach and Landing

20. Mislanding

21. After Landing

22. Fuel Capacities and Consumption

23. Beam Approach

Revised in Vol. I by A.L.42
and In Pilot's Notes by A.L./P.

AIR PUBLICATION 1564B & D
Volume I and Pilot's Notes.

SECTION 2

HANDLING AND FLYING NOTES FOR PILOT

1. ENGINE DATA: MERLIN XX

   (i) Fuel: 100 octane only

  (ii) Oil: See A.P. 1464/C.37

 (iii) Engine limitations:

		R.p.m.	Boost lb./sq.in.	Temp. $^{\circ}$C Clnt.	Oil
MAX. TAKE-OFF TO 1,000 FEET	M	3,000	+12	-	-
MAX. CLIMBING 1 HR. LIMIT	M) S)	2,850	+9	125	90
MAX. RICH CONTINUOUS	M) S)	2,650	+7	105*	90
MAX. WEAK CONTINUOUS	M) S)	2,650	+4	105^{1}	90
COMBAT 5 MINS. LIMIT	M S	3,000 3,000	+14* +16*	135 135	105 105

Note:

* Combat boost is obtained by operating the boost
control cut-out.

1 115°C coolant temperature is permitted for short
periods at cruising rpm.

OIL PRESSURE: NORMAL: 60-80 lb./sq.in.
                     MINIMUM: 45

MINM. TEMP. FOR TAKE-OFF:OIL: 15°C
                    COOLANT: 60°C

FUEL PRESSURE: 8-10 lb./sq.in.

F.S/1

2. FLYING LIMITATIONS

  (i) <u>Maximum speeds (mph IAS)</u>:

Diving:	390
Undercarriage down:	120
Flaps down:	120

  (ii) At AUWs in excess of 8,750 lb. care is necessary in ground handling and the aircraft should be taken off only from concrete or equivalent runways.

 (iii) Spinning is probibited at all times of Mark IID and IV aircraft, and of Mark IIA, B and C aircraft only when carrying 90-gallon drop tanks, bombs, SCI, containers, or RP.

  (iv) Aerobatics are prohibited and violent manoeuvres must be avoided when carrying 90-gallon drop tanks, bombs, SCI, containers, or RP (Mk IIA, B and C aircraft only).

  (v) Aircraft carrying drop tanks should not be dived.

  (vi) Mark III containers must not be dropped at speeds in excess of 150 mph IAS and at heights lower than 500 feet.

 (vii) Bombs should be jettisoned and RP fired, if possible, before landing.

3. POSITION ERROR CORRECTIONS

From To	100 120	120 150	150 180	180 210	210 270	270 320	mph IAS mph IAS
Add Subtract	4	2	0 0	2	4	6	mph mph

4. MANAGEMENT OF FUEL AND OIL SYSTEMS

  (i) The Main Tanks should be used first, but if the Reserve Tank is used before the Main Tanks, the following precautions must be observed:

    (a) Change over to MAIN TANKS ON before emptying the Reserve Tank.

    (b) If this has not been done and the engine cuts, close the throttle (to avoid over-revving when the engine picks up) and change over to MAIN TANKS ON <u>at once</u>.

Revised in Vol. I by A.L.42
and in Pilot's Notes by A.L/P.

A.P. 1564B & D Sect. 2
Volume I and Pilot's Notes.

(c)   In order to displace air drawn into the fuel system from the empty reserve tank, the engine must be windmilled at high speed, when it will pick up after a few seconds. It is emphasised that the pick-up will not be immediate after the change-over.

(ii)   If fitted with fixed auxiliary tanks:

(a)   Start and take-off in the normal way on the main tanks.

(b)   As soon as the contents gauge registers only 5 gallons in the main tanks, switch ON the auxiliary tank pumps.

(c)   Switch OFF the pumps immediately the contents gauge registers 25 gallons.

(d)   When the contents of the MAIN TANKS are again reduced to 5 gallons, switch ON the pumps until the contents gauge again registers 25 gallons and then switch OFF the pumps. The auxiliary tanks will then be practically empty.

(iii)   If fitted with drop tanks:

(a)   Start and take-off in the normal way on the main tanks.

(b)   At a safe height (say 2,000 feet) change over to a drop tank and turn the pressurising cock to PRESSURE. Turn OFF the main tanks.

(c)   When the drop tank is empty and the fuel pressure warning light comes on, change-over to the second drop tank and at the same time turn ON the reserve tank, which should still be full. This will enable the engine to pick up more quickly and when it does so turn OFF the reserve tank and change-over to the second drop tank.

(d)   When the second drop tank is empty and the fuel pressure warning light comes on, turn ON the main tanks and turn OFF the drop tank. If the engine does not pick up on the main tanks, prime the system by using the reserve tank as before.

F.S/2

(e)   The cock for the auxiliary oil tank (if fitted) should be turned on about $3\frac{1}{2}$ hours after take-off, but not before this time. After having been turned on, the cock cannot afterwards be turned off during flight.

(f)   On reinforcing flights, under maximum range engine conditions (2,650 rpm and +4 lb./sq.in. boost on climb to height, and level flight at 190 mph IAS reducing to 160 mph IAS after jettisoning tanks) oil consumption is considerably reduced and, therefore, the auxiliary oil tank should not be turned on until after approximately 5 hours flight, when there will be sufficient space in the main tank to accommodate the extra 4 gallons. The normal oil tank should be filled to 8 gallons only.

5.   PRELIMINARIES

(i)   If fitted with R.P. and a drop tank or R.P. and a bomb, the aircraft should be trimmed carefully to relieve stick load.

The recommended aileron tab setting is neutral at full load. Then with a drop tank fitted under the port wing, changes in load will cause the following alterations in trim:

Tank empty:	Slightly right wing low
Tank empty and RP fired:	Trim satisfactory
Tank jettisoned and RP fired:	Slightly right wing low
Tank jettisoned, RP not fired:	Right wing low

(ii)   Switch on the undercarriage indicator and check green lights. Test the change-over switch.

(iii)   See that the short (lower) arm of the hydraulic selector safety catch is across the wheels up slot of the gate.

(iv)   Check that the throttle pushbutton master switch is OFF.

(v)   Check contents of fuel tanks. If fitted with auxiliary tanks see that the pump switches or cock control are OFF.

(vi)   Test operation of flying controls.

(vii)   See that the cockpit hood is locked open.

Revised in Vol. I by A.L.42   A.P. 1564B & D Sect. 2
and in Pilot's Notes by A.L/P.   Volume I and Pilot's Notes.

6. STARTING THE ENGINE AND WARMING UP

    (i)   Set fuel cock to MAIN TANKS ON.

    (ii) Set the controls as follows:

                    Throttle   - ½ inch open

                    Propeler control - fully forward

                    Supercharger control - MODERATE

                    Radiator shutter - OPEN

    (iii) If an external priming connection is fitted, high
          volatility fuel (Stores Ref. 34A/111) should be used
          for priming at air temperatures below freezing. Work
          the priming pump until the fuel reaches the priming
          nozzles; this may be judged by a sudden increase in
          resistance.

    (iv) Switch ON the ignition and press the starter and booster
          coil pushbuttons. Turning periods must not exceed 20
          seconds, with a 30 seconds wait between each. Work
          the priming pump as rapidly and vigorously as possible
          while the engine is being turned; it should start after
          the following number of strokes if cold:

Air temperature °C:	+30	+20	+10	0	-10	-20
Normal fuel:	3	4	7	12		
High volatility fuel:				4	8	18

    (v)   At temperatures below freezing it will probably be
          necessary to continue priming after the engine has fired
          and until it picks up on the carburettor.

    (vi) Release the starter button as soon as the engine starts
          and as soon as it is running satisfactorily release the
          booster coil pushbutton and screw down the priming pump.

    (vii) Open up slowly to 1,000 rpm, then warm up at this speed.

7. TESTING THE ENGINE AND INSTALLATIONS

    While warming up:

    (i)   Check temperatures and pressures, and test operation
          of hydraulic system by lowering and raising the flaps.

F.S/3

After warming up, with two men on the tail:

Note: The following tests consitute a comprehensive check
to be carried out after inspection or repair, or at
the pilot's discretion. In normal circumstances they
may be reduced in accordance with local instructions.

(ii)   Open up to +4 lb./sq.in. boost and exercise and check
operation of the two speed supercharger. Rpm should fall
when S ratio is engaged.

(iii) At +4 lb./sq.in. boost exercise and check operation of
the constant speed propeller. Rpm should fall to 1,800
with the control fully back. Check that the generator
is charging; the power failure light should be out and
the voltage 14 or over.

(iv)   With the propeller control fully forward open the
throttle up to +12 lb./sq.in. boost and check static
boost and rpm which should be 3,000.

(v)   Throttle back to +9 lb./sq.in. boost and test each
magneto in turn. The drop should not exceed 150 rpm.

(vi)   Before taxying check brake pressure (100 lb./sq in.
minm.) and pneumatic supply pressure (220 lb./sq.in.)

8. CHECK LIST BEFORE TAKE-OFF

T -	Trimming tabs	- Rudder: Fully right
		Elevator: Nautral
P -	Propeller control -	Fully forward
F -	Fuel	- Check contents of main tanks
		- MAIN TANKS ON
		- Aux. tank cock or pumps - OFF
		- Pressuring cock - ATMOSPHERE
F -	Flaps	- UP (28° down - two divs. on
		indicator - for shortest take-off run)
	Supercharger control	- MODERATE
	Radiator shutter	- Fully OPEN

9. TAKE-OFF

(i)   Open the throttle slowly to the gate, or fully if full
take-off boost is necessary.

(ii)   Any tendency to swing can be counteracted by the rudder.
When fitted with 2 x 500 lb. bombs the tendency to swing
left is slightly more pronounced.

Revised in Vol. I by A.L.42   A.P. 1564B & D Sect. 2
and in Pilot's Notes by A.L/P.   Volume I and Pilot's Notes.

(iii) After raising the undercarriage return the selector
       lever to neutral and retrim nose heavy.

(iv)   Do not start to climb before a speed of 140 mph IAS
       is attained.

10. CLIMBING

(i)   The speeds for maximum rate of climb are as follows:

       Up to 16,000 feet: 140 mph IAS
       At 21,000 feet: 135 mph IAS
       At 26,000 feet: 130 mph IAS
       At 31,000 feet: 125 mph IAS

       Change to S ratio when the boost has fallen by 5 lb./
       sq.in.
       At full load 155 mph IAS is the most comfortable
       climbing speed.
       Considerable surging may be experienced above 8,000 feet
       on aircraft on which the air intake duct has been removed.

(ii)   When fitted with 2 x 90-gallon drop tanks the aircraft
       are longitudinally unstable on the climb.

(iii) When fitted with 2 x 500 lb. bombs there is a similar
       tendency to pitch if the rudder is not held steady.

(iv)   The fuel tank pressure control should normally be kept
       to ATMOSPHERE (except when required to supply fuel
       from the drop tanks), but should be turned on (PRESSURE)
       if the fuel pressure warning light comes on.

11. GENERAL FLYING

(i)   Stability: The aircraft are normally just stable
       longitudinally, but when carrying 90-gallon drop
       tanks, or R.P. and one 90-gallon drop tank, they
       become unstable longitudinally and, in the first
       case, 190 mph IAS is the minimum comfortable flying
       speed. In conditions of absolute calm this can be
       reduced to 180 mph IAS. When carrying bombs, R.P. or
       containers, longitudinal stability is unaffected.

F.S/4

(ii)   Change of trim:

        Undercarriage down   -   Nose slightly down

        Flaps down   -   Nose down

(iii) In steep turns there is a tendency to tighten up.

(iv)   In bad visibility near the ground, flaps should be lowered to about 40° (3 divisions) and the propeller speed control set to give 2,650 rpm. Speed may then be reduced to about 110 mph IAS. The radiator shutter must be opened to keep the temperature at about 100°C.

(v)   When operating in tropical conditions prolonged flying at maximum cruising power should be avoided when top speed is not essential.

12. MAXIMUM PERFORMANCE

(i)   Climbing:

See Para. 10(i).

(ii)   Combat:

Use S ratio if the boost in M ratio is 2 lb./sq.in. below the maximum permitted.

13. ECONOMICAL FLYING

(i)   Climbing: Climb at 2,850 rpm and +9 lb./sq.in. boost at the speeds recommended for maximum rate of climb (See Para. 10).

(ii)   Cruising: For maximum range fly in M ratio and at maximum obtainable boost not exceeding +4 lb./sq.in. and reduce speed by reducing rpm which may be as low as 1,800, but check that the generator is charging. On some early aircraft it will not do so at below 2,000 rpm. If at 1,800 rpm (or 2,000 if necessary) the speed is higher than that recommended, reduce boost.

S ratio should only be used if at 2,600 rpm the recommended speed cannot be obtained in M ratio.

Revised in Vol. I by A.L.42   A.P. 1564B & D Sect. 2
and in Pilot's Notes by A.L/P.   Volume I and Pilot's Notes.

   (iii)   The recommended speeds (mph IAS) for maximum range
           are:

Standard aircraft:	160
When fitted with 2 x 44 or 45 gal. tanks	160
When fitted with 2 x 90 gal. tanks	170 or as near as possible
When fitted with 2 x 250 lb. bombs	170
When fitted with 2 x 500 lb. bombs	180

14. STALLING

   (i)   At the stall one wing usually drops sharply, often
        over the vertical, with flaps either up or down.

   (ii)   The average stalling speeds (mph IAS) for the aircraft
        at various AUW (from 7,600 lbs. to 9,200 lbs.) are:

Undercarriage and flaps UP:	80-90
Undercarriage and flaps DOWN:	60-75

The speeds for individual aircraft may vary by 5 mph.

15. SPINNING

   (i)   Spinning of Mk IID and Mk IV aircraft is prohibited
        at all times.

   (ii)   On Mark IIA, B and C aircraft spinning is prohibited
        when carrying 90-gallon drop tanks, bombs, SCI or R.P.

   (iii)   Recovery is normal, but the loss of height involved
        in recovery may be very great and the following limits
        are to be observed:

        (a)   Spins are not to be started below 10,000 feet.

        (b)   Recovery is to be initiated before two turns are
           completed.

   (iv)   A speed of 150 mph IAS should be attained before
        starting to ease out of the resultant dive.

F.S/5

16. AEROBATICS

   (i) The following speeds are recommended:

Loop:	At least 280 mph IAS
Roll:	220-250 mph IAS
Half roll off loop:	At least 300 mph IAS
Upward roll:	300 mph IAS

17. DIVING

   (i) Speed builds up slowly in the dive and the aircraft becomes tail heavy as the speed increases. The elevator trimming tabs should be used with care.

  (ii) Care should be taken not to allow the aircraft to yaw to the right, as this produces a marked nosedown pitching tendency.

 (iii) If fitted with Bombs, S.C.I., or containers, the aircraft should be eased out of the dive gently. If fitted with drop tanks it should not be dived.

18. CHECK LIST BEFORE LANDING

   (i) Check brake pressure (100 lbs./sq.in. minm.).

  (ii) Reduce speed to 120 mph IAS and check that cockpit hood is locked open.

U - Undercarriage	-	DOWN (check green lights)
P - Propeller control	-	Fully forward
Supercharger control	-	MODERATE
F - Flaps	-	DOWN

19. APPROACH AND LANDING

   (i) Approach speeds (mph IAS) at normal load:

		flaps up
Engine assisted:	95	(105)
Glide:	105	(115)

Note: If carrying drop tanks, bombs, or R.P., the normal engine assisted approach should be made at about 110 mph IAS.

Revised in Vol. I by A.L.42
and in Pilot's Notes by A.L/P

A.P. 1564B & D. Sect. 2
Volume I and Pilot's Notes.

(ii) <u>Undercarriage</u>: The lever should have been left in
neutral, but if it has been left in the UP position,
be careful to disengage the thumb catch by easing the
selector lever forward before trying to move it to the
DOWN position, otherwise the lever may become jammed.
Return the lever to neutral as soon as the undercarriage
is down.

(iii) <u>Flaps</u>: If 120 mph IAS is exceeded with the flaps fully
down, they will be partially raised by the airflow.
They will automatically move to the fully down position
when speed is reduced sufficiently provided that the
selector lever is left at DOWN.

(iv) Landing with R.P. only on one wing should be made at
as high a speed as possible and care must be taken to
counteract dropping of the wing.

20. MISLANDING

(i) Raise the undercarriage immediately.

(ii) Climb at about 90 mph IAS.

(iii) Raise the flaps at a safe height of about 200-300 feet,
at a speed of not less than 120 mph IAS.

(iv) With one 500 lb. bomb stuck up open the throttle slowly
and speed on the initial climb should be 110 mph IAS
before raising flaps at 120 mph IAS.

21. AFTER LANDING

(i) Raise the flaps before taxying.

(ii) To stop the engine, idle for ½ minute at 800-900 rpm,
then pull the slow-running cut-out and hold it out
until the engine stops.

(iii) Turn OFF the fuel cock and switch OFF the ignition.

(iv) Check that the hydraulic selector safety plate is
covering the WHEELS UP position.

(v) <u>Oil dilution</u>: (See A.P. 2095 Pilot's Notes General).
The correct dilution period for these aircraft is:

Atmospheric temperature above -10°C: 1 minute
Atmospheric temperature below -10°C: 2 minutes

F.S/6

22. FUEL CAPACITIES AND CONSUMPTION

   (i) <u>Fuel capacities</u>:

   (a) <u>Normal</u>:

Two Main Tanks (33 gals. each):	66 gallons
One Reserve tank:	28 gallons
Total :	94 gallons

   (b) <u>Long-range (totals)</u>:

With 2 fixed under-wing tanks (44 gallons each):	<u>182 gallons</u>
With 2 x 45 gallon drop tanks:	<u>184 gallons</u>
With 2 x 90 gallon drop tanks:	<u>274 gallons</u>

(ii) The approximate consumptions (gals/hr.) in WEAK mixture are as follows:

Boost lbs./ sq.in.	M ratio at 8,000 - 20,000 ft.			S ratio at 14,000 - 30,000 ft.		
	R.p.m.			R.p.m.		
	2,650	2,300	2,000	2,650	2,300	2,000
+4	56	50	46	57	51	47
+2	52	46	42	53	47	43
0	47	42	38	48	43	39
-2	42	37	34	43	39	35
-4	37	33	30	38	34	31

(iii) The approximate consumptions in RICH mixture are as follows:

R.p.m.	Boost lb./sq.in.	Galls/hr.
3,000	+12	115
3,000	+9	100
2,850	+9	95
2,650	+7	80

127

Revised in Vol. I by A.L. 42
and in Pilot's Notes by A.L./P.

A.P. 1564B & D. Sect. 2
Volume I and Pilot's Notes.

23. BEAM APPROACH

STAGE	Indicated height (feet)*	I.A.S. m.p.h.	R.p.m.	Approx. Boost	Actions	Change of Trim and Remarks
PRELIMINARY APPROACH	1,500	120	2,400	-2	Flaps down 30°C	Strongly nose down
	1,500	120	2,400	-1	Lower u/c on QDR over IMB	Slightly nose down
AT OUTER MARKER BEACON	600	95-100	3,000	-4	Flaps down to 60°	Nose down
			3,000	0		Should give level flight
AT INNER MARKER BEACON	100	90-95	3,000			
OVERSHOOT	Up to 400	95-100	3,000	Full throttle	Raise u/c and retrim.	Nose up
					Raise flap to 30°C and retrim.	Nose up
					Raise flaps fully and retrim.	Nose up
					Adjust boost and rpm at 1,000 feet.	

* Altimeter adjusted for Q.F.E. and touch down error as follows:
At take-off, with no flap, the altimeter reads - 30 feet.
At touch-down, with 60° flap, the altimeter reads -55 feet.
so add two millibars to Q.F.E. to give zero reading at touch-down.

Note:
The above speeds should be increased by 5 mph for Mark IID and IV aircraft.